Additional Praise for The Complete Guide to Knowledge Management

"Whether an expert or neophyte in KM, you will benefit from the trusted insights of Pasher and Ronen. Few have as much practical perspective into the art and science of this new functional discipline. Each chapter is a gem—complete with the Magnificent 7 insights which fuse the tactical and strategic, the theory and the practice, from idea to action. They have captured the kaleidoscopic landscape of intangible value and intellectual wealth into a strategy leading to innovation progress—the true competence of the decade."

—Debra M. Amidon, Founder of ENTOVATION International Ltd;
author of *The Innovation Superhighway*

"As a member of the community of practice in the field of knowledge management and dissemination, I am pleased to take the tools offered in this book to my colleagues in higher education. The combination of theory and practice presented in the book serves for us as a springboard to real-life leadership positions."

—Professor Nava Ben-Zvi, PhD, President of
Hadassah College, Jerusalem

"This is a deeply innovative and practical book. Pasher and Ronen merge the core competencies of knowledge creation with those of management to deliver competitive advantage for the twenty-first century."

—Glenda Eoyang, founding Executive Director
of the Human Systems Dynamics Institute

"Through learning landscapes, case-tellers, 'Magnificent 7' summaries, and the like, Edna and Tuvya's *Complete Guide to Knowledge Management* leads you to a richly contextualized universe of knowledge-creation possibilities. Indeed, this book will challenge you personally to step into an assertive, resilient, and empowered knowledge-based lifestyle!"

—Blanca Garcia, *Most Admired Knowledge City Awards*;
Chair of The World Capital Institute

"This book excels by helping managers to understand and practice the social, cultural, and also the dynamic nature of knowledge in enterprises, and of their customers. This approach really defines the mechanisms of a knowledge society!"

—Dr. Otthein Herzog, Professor and CEO of
InnovationsKontor Nordwest GmbH

"What I really enjoyed when reading this book were the great many examples that reminded me of situations I have experienced during my occupational career. But it also brought forward new ideas to me for my business. This book should be all-in-one a must read for those at the beginning of their careers."

—Dr. Michael Lawo, Professor and Managing Director of
Mobile-Solution Group GmbH, Bremen, Germany

"Bravo! At last, a practical and down-to-earth approach to KM, rich both in concrete examples and in challenging insights (like the 'Magnificent 7' at the end of each chapter)."

—Dr. Charles M. Savage, author of *Fifth Generation Management*

"I found the book very unique and useful. The fusion of the different perspectives of the authors—a manager and a management consultant—and the fusion of theory with practice make it interesting to read and easy to use. As an Israeli manager, I am of course made very happy and proud by a book full of Israeli examples—especially those from RAFAEL, a leading R&D organization."

—Major General (Ret.) Amiaz Sagis, Former Head of the Technology
and Logistics Division in the Israel Defense Forces (IDF);
CEO and Chairman of the Board of large Israeli corporations

The Complete Guide to Knowledge Management

The Complete Guide to Knowledge Management

A Strategic Plan to Leverage Your Company's Intellectual Capital

EDNA PASHER AND TUVYA RONEN

WILEY

John Wiley & Sons, Inc.

Published by John Wiley & Sons, Inc., Hoboken, New Jersey.
Published simultaneously in Canada.

Library of Congress Cataloging-in-Publication Data

Pasher, Edna.
   The complete guide to knowledge management : a strategic plan to leverage your company's intellectual capital / Edna Pasher and Tuvya Ronen.
      p. cm.
   Includes index.
   ISBN 978-0-470-88129-3 (hardback); ISBN 978-1-118-00140-0 (ebk);
ISBN 978-1-118-00139-4 (ebk); ISBN 978-1-118-00138-7 (ebk)
   1. Knowledge management.   2. Intellectual capital–Management.   I. Ronen, Tuvya. II. Title.
   HD30.2.P375 2011
   658.4'038–dc22

                                                                    2010051230

Printed in the United States of America

10 9 8 7 6 5 4 3 2 1

To Margalit, whose love, patience, and wisdom
accompanied me in this journey for Knowledge
Management as in all our travels on the roads of life.

—Tuvya

To Yossi Pasher, who has been supporting me
to grow our intellectual capital and make
my dreams come true, with love.

—Edna

Contents

Acknowledgments

We thank all of our friends in the Intellectual Capital Pioneers community, who opened our eyes to new possibilities.

—Edna

I would like to thank the people of Rafael, my mentors, colleagues, and personal friends during my professional career. Their friendship, dedication, and knowledge were the inspiration for this book. I began this knowledge management journey to bring us some of the lessons learned in the outside world, to find that we have much of our own to contribute to others.

 I especially thank those Rafael's people, too many to mention by name, who were either the sources of various examples or helped in reviewing parts of the manuscript.

 I am grateful to my Ph.D. advisor, Professor Arthur Bryson from Stanford University, for inspiring my engineering work as well as being a role model of knowledge creating and sharing.

—Tuvya

We would like to thank Ruth Blatt, with whom we wrote the first version of this book.

 We are grateful to Lynne Rabinoff, our literary agent, who found a home for our manuscript at John Wiley & Sons. In this home, we thank Susan McDermott and Claire Wesley, and we especially appreciate the great contribution of our development editor, Jennifer MacDonald, whose expertise, patience, and dedication transformed the manuscript into a real book.

—Edna and Tuvya

Preface

Getting Started on Your
Knowledge Management Journey

Welcome to the beginning of your knowledge management (KM) journey. On this journey, you will travel with us, Tuvya and Edna, two KM experts searching for successful solutions to various KM issues in all types of markets and situations. This book takes the intangible and abstract topic of KM and makes it concrete and applicable.

Most managers already know something about KM and are curious to learn more, but their initial backgrounds may differ considerably: Many have only heard *knowledge management* used as a buzzword; some may hold the common misconception that it is only about systematically recording existing knowledge; and still others have already realized its strategic value. All of them, however, share a common goal that renders them prospective experts: to fully understand KM, to know their role in implementing it, and to acquire the necessary skills and tools for doing it successfully.

A Book for Managers

This book is intended to prepare managers to be the leaders of KM in their organizations. The continuous growth of knowledge, the most important core competence of the modern organization, ensures the long-term growth and profit of an organization. Managers at all levels of the organization must be the leaders and catalysts of KM. It is the manager who must comprehend and exploit the strategic significance of knowledge by· instilling the processes of knowledge creating and knowledge sharing in an organization's culture and, in particular, continually fostering innovation.

While managers must learn to be KM leaders, most books on the subject do not address their special needs. This book aims to fill that gap. It addresses all manners of KM topics and takes managers on an intellectual journey into knowledge management.

We begin our journey by establishing the business case to justify KM as a tool to increase the *intangible* asset of intellectual capital, which in turn ensures the *tangible* assets of future financial success. We then link strategy and knowledge management, and describe how to establish an appropriate KM culture geared toward constantly creating new knowledge.

We then take the manager along through a variety of focuses that represent the different topics of knowledge management, from the human aspects of managing knowledge workers, promoting interactions for knowledge creating and sharing, to knowledge-capturing processes, exploiting customer knowledge, and measuring the performance of increasing intellectual capital.

The peak of our journey involves knowledge renewal and the role of the manager in fostering innovation (the new use of existing knowledge and the creation of new knowledge).

Introducing the Authors

As authors, our background is particularly suited to understanding and fulfilling the unique needs of managers engaging in knowledge management. Dr. Tuvya Ronen is a vice president at Rafael, a leading aerospace company in Israel, where he gained extensive experience in managing research and development teams in projects and in professional departments. Dr. Edna Pasher is a strategic management consultant, an international pioneer in the intellectual capital community, and a leader in implementing knowledge management in Israeli organizations. We both have extensive experience in practicing knowledge management in organizations and have gained a deep familiarity with cutting-edge developments on the subject. While we have teamed together in writing this book, we represent different but complementing experience and perspectives.

Moreover, throughout the book, we also contribute our unique experience as authors, managers, and consultants living and working in the country of Israel, a small country always struggling to compensate for its lack of physical resources by utilizing successful KM strategies. In recent years Israel has established itself as a knowledge country, with economic success. The land of "the People of the Book" is now commonly referred to as "the Second Silicon Valley" or "the Start-Up Nation." Israel was one of the first countries to emerge from the 2008–2009 world financial crisis.

There is a growing interest in its story of successful KM on a national level, and Edna is often invited to tell this story at international KM conferences. We therefore have many examples to share from the Israeli history of excellence in creating intellectual capital (IC) out of KM.

In particular, Tuvya's experience at Rafael has proven striking in providing examples for this book. Rafael has intuitively created a legacy of KM practices that began during a time when the term had not even been invented. The stories we present here from Rafael and Israel, combined with the other extensive global examples, create a comprehensive assembly of numerous nonstandard cases that managers can analyze and utilize. These cases include both large and small companies and are likely to be relevant and refreshing for readers (even those who already have some experience in KM).

Each of us experienced, in his own field, the major consequences of the two most recent economic bubbles: the first in early 2000 and the last beginning in 2008. We make a point of discussing KM examples as influenced by these bubbles.

How This Book Is Organized

We have structured this book to help you understand and implement a systematic and comprehensive knowledge management process. The chapters guide you in this journey, and—except when indicated otherwise—are helpful to read in order of appearance.

The KM journey follows a spiral path, as shown in Figure P.1. It does not terminate at the peak, since effective knowledge management is a continuous and never-ending process; rather, the end is a new beginning in a continuous journey, leading an organization to ever-higher peaks. Figure P.1 depicts the four phases of this journey, which we describe as follows.

Phase 1: Hitting the Road

This book begins with Chapter 1, "The Motivation toward Knowledge Management: Combining the Tactical with the Strategic," which presents the basic managerial catalysts for the journey into knowledge management: the questions, issues, and solutions involved. Most managers acquire their interest in KM while discovering tactical KM problems of knowledge capturing and knowledge sharing. They later realize the strategic importance of knowledge as the basic asset of the modern organization. In this chapter, we discuss both the tactical and strategic aspects of KM by providing easy-to-follow examples.

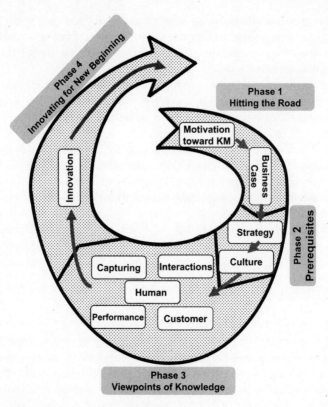

FIGURE P.1 The Knowledge Management Journey

Chapter 2, "Making the Business Case for Managing Intellectual Capital," explains how a manager can solidify the business rationale for investing time and money in knowledge management. Knowledge management aims to increase the tangible assets of an organization by increasing its intangible assets (the intellectual capital).

Phase 2: Prerequisites

Prior to starting the journey to successful knowledge management, managers and organizations must consider two essential prerequisites. First, managers must establish a comprehensive business strategy (composed of a vision, a mission, and a strategy to implement it) and knowledge management must serve that strategy. Chapter 3, "The Importance of Strategy in Knowledge Management," emphasizes the tight coupling between knowledge management and strategy.

Second, knowledge management hinges on developing a system of shared values and a management style that seeks and develops an employee's knowledge. This management style is based on a culture of trust, innovation, and respect for the knowledge of the workers. Chapter 4, "The Role of Culture in a Successful Knowledge-Creating and Knowledge-Sharing Organization," explains and advocates these cultural requirements.

Phase 3: Viewpoints of Knowledge

Phase 3 presents critical viewpoints on knowledge management that you should consider for your organization. Chapter 5, "The Human Focus: Understanding and Managing Knowledge Workers," discusses how the success of a knowledge company is based on the proper management of its knowledge workers. It shows how to make an organization attractive to knowledge workers so that they will be motivated to join the organization and stay with it. It describes tools for enlarging the workers' knowledge and encouraging them to contribute their knowledge to a management process. This chapter is distinguished from the abundance of literature on human resource management in that it focuses specifically on knowledge issues and knowledge workers. We analyze lessons learned from the two bubble economies on successfully managing, attracting, and retaining knowledge workers and their knowledge.

Chapter 6, "Managing Interactions for Knowledge Creation and Sharing," discusses how knowledge is created and shared largely by social interactions. This chapter provides readers with methods to promote positive interactions to foster knowledge-creating and knowledge-sharing communities in their organizations. It provides a detailed discussion of formal and informal techniques that provide the cultural and physical environment for these communities to prosper.

Chapter 7, "Capturing and Reusing Knowledge," presents methods for capturing and codifying existing knowledge in the organization and making it available to any number of potential users.

Chapter 8, "The Customer Focus: Harnessing Customer Knowledge through Meaningful Interactions," presents opportunities and methods for making customers partners in creating knowledge and in shaping an organization's future. As the chapter details, customers possess a lot of valuable knowledge and are often willing to share it if an organization has the will and resources to inquire, and to co-create knowledge with them.

Chapter 9, "Measuring and Managing the Performance of Proper Knowledge Work," provides readers with the appropriate measurement systems required for effective knowledge management of the intangible asset of intellectual capital. These are added to the classical accounting methods indispensable for effective management of tangible resources.

Phase 4: Innovating for a New Beginning

In Chapter 10, "Innovating for a New Beginning," the journey has one mandatory stop before it can begin anew: knowledge creation through innovation. Constant innovation in all business activities is a must for the continuous survival of an organization. This chapter describes various techniques for fostering a culture that encourages and enables workers to innovate.

And finally, the last chapter, "Conclusion: Implementing Knowledge Management—A Step-by-Step Process," outlines practical steps for readers to begin to implement proper knowledge management, particularly identifying where and how to begin the process in one's own organization.

Notes on Style

Before concluding this preface, we would like to draw the readers' attention to some particular styles used throughout the book:

Referencing the Authors and Sources

Our policy in referring to us, the authors, represents our combined message as well as our different perspectives. We usually refer to ourselves in first person as "we." However, in many cases we refer to "Tuvya" or "Edna" in the third-person. This is done mainly to emphasize his or her particular experience or point of view, but sometimes even to present disagreements between us.

We have two different policies in referring to people mentioned in the various examples. In cases based on interviews with managers and KM experts, or on written sources, we make every effort to cite them accurately with their name and their title at the time of interview. In other cases based on our personal experience, where people are mentioned without being interviewed, we substitute first names to respect their privacy. In both cases, any interpretation is our responsibility.

Definition of Knowledge and Intellectual Capital

This book is about knowledge and intellectual capital, and we have used these terms freely without asserting exact definitions. While expecting the context and your experience to make them clear, we offer this simplified definition: *Knowledge* is the experience and expertise that, when combined with basic data and information (which are not discussed here), can solve problems and create value. This value is the *intellectual capital*.

More thorough definitions of these basic terms (data, information, knowledge, intellectual capital, and wisdom) are quickly described in the Appendix at the back of this book. This appendix may also serve as an alternate approach for introducing the subject.

Conclusion

When you have read all the chapters of this book you will have a complete guide to knowledge management. Next, you are able to start implementing the different methods you learned in your organization (or department, or team—remember that KM can be used at any level!). Our hope is that this book will take you all the way from strategy to implementation and that you will see the very tangible results of success in a number of ways. To that end, each chapter finishes with a list of seven guidelines (which we call "The Magnificent 7") to help you remember the most important points of the chapter's subject.

Good luck!

CHAPTER 1

The Motivation toward Knowledge Management

Combining the Tactical with the Strategic

In this chapter you will:

- Review examples of typical tactical knowledge management problems.
- Discover how knowledge management is actually a strategic tool aiming to increase the intellectual capital essential for long-term success of an organization.
- Learn that the manager should lead knowledge management efforts in an organization because of its importance as a procedural tool with both tactical and strategic relevance to success.

Most managers, when they begin this journey into knowledge management (KM), do not even know what knowledge management entails. They are only familiar with some of its problems from their day-to-day experience with the flow of knowledge in their organization. These day-to-day experiences are considered *tactical*, meaning they interfere with an organization's efficiency and performance. An example of a tactical issue might be that a manager notices a worker or colleague is not open to sharing his position's knowledge, so the manager needs to reinvent processes that already exist.

Later, when managers become more involved in learning about successful knowledge management, they realize the tactical problems also have *strategic* implications and solutions that can further the intellectual capital of their organization overall. For instance, modern high-tech organizations use KM to align their research and development (R&D) efforts. Or traditional industries realize that KM helps them use their current core competencies, or develop new ones, in order to quickly invest in new products, services, and solutions that the market needs. Simply put, effective KM will turn any organization into a fast-learning one, geared toward a sustained, competitive advantage.

Once managers realize how important knowledge management is overall, they begin looking for help but often are not sure how to implement the proper plan.

This chapter begins with an account of some of the challenges that led the authors on their personal KM journeys. The challenges described here use examples of KM problems, all of which are typical of what readers might encounter in their business. The chapter continues with responses to these challenges and ends with some universal truths about KM issues, paving the way to the more detailed discussions found throughout this book.

A Manager Struggling with Key *Tactical* Problems

Co-author Tuvya Ronen became aware of KM problems in the late 1990s. Tuvya is now a vice president at Rafael Advanced Defense Systems Ltd., where he manages an R&D center of about 1,500 engineers and scientists. Rafael is a leading aerospace company in Israel—with $1.6 billion in annual sales and about 6,000 employees—whose products are based on an intensive use of innovative R&D. Tuvya has spent most of his career at Rafael.

Basically, the goal of an R&D center at Rafael, as in any organization, is to create and disseminate knowledge. Unknowingly, Rafael has established a unique knowledge culture that utilizes several first-class KM methods. However, some changes over the course of Tuvya's time at Rafael have challenged its ability to increase efficiency and competitiveness. To his dismay, Tuvya found that this was an ongoing process: New knowledge problems were always emerging where none existed before.

The following examples describe some typical problems that Tuvya first encountered in the late 1990s, when he was managing one of the departments of the R&D center at Rafael.

Ben's Bright Idea Surprisingly Rejected

Ben is a leading member of a team of aerodynamic designers. Their work requires using several different codes for estimating aerodynamic properties, such as lift and drag. Ben made an obvious and simple suggestion: Whenever somebody uses a code, he should write comments detailing the experience. These comments would be useful for others: determining which code suits a specific family of configurations or flight velocity, bug alerts, and so on.

In the old days, this suggestion would have been hailed by workers and managers alike. Surprisingly, objections sprang up like mushrooms after the rain: Why would an employee want to spend time for the benefit of others when tight schedules and deadlines pull him back to his work? When and why would coworkers read the comments? Who would sponsor the extra work? Where would the money come from in light of tight budgets and narrow profit margins?

The main issue presented in this example is: How can employees learn from each other when they don't have the time, money, or managerial attention? Is Ben's idea the best solution? Are there other, better solutions?

Nathan, the Irreplaceable Technician

Nathan is a veteran technician but the organization decided to encourage him to seek early retirement. The situation seemed win-win: He would enjoy a generous retirement package and his department could replace a not-so-cutting-edge technician with an aspiring, young engineer.

Unexpectedly, it turned out that Nathan was irreplaceable as he was the sole source of knowledge in his position. Specifically, only he knew how to maintain an old simulator that was essential to the department's work. Before the decision to ask him to retire, his coworkers had no interest in the old simulator with outdated technology so they did not hasten to acquire his knowledge before encouraging his retirement.

The main issue presented in this example is: How can an organization avoid a situation whereby a single person holds all the knowledge about a key subject?

Ron's Knowledge Leaving the Organization

Ron is a senior veteran engineer who has held various management positions. Through the years he has become a walking encyclopedia about the design and operation of a family of products. Everybody likes

(continued)

to hear his view. Even younger engineers, who consider him old-fashioned, ask for his advice if only to do the opposite.

In the old days, everybody knew about Ron, and felt he would always be a part of the organization. Nowadays, his fame has declined and many people do not know about his expertise. He may even retire or move to another organization.

The main issues presented in this example are: Can Ron's knowledge about existing products be documented? Is it possible to create an expert system, using the knowledge of Ron and others, to advise us about new projects? How do we identify important sources like Ron for other workers to use? Are there similar useful sources hidden from the other workers' experience?

Tuvya assumed that he was not the first person to encounter these types of knowledge issues within an organization. He wanted to find out how other organizations, both in Israel and globally, had solved them. He decided to dedicate a generous amount of time to searching for successful answers and will share many of them with you throughout this book.

A Consultant Struggling with Key *Strategic* Problems

During Tuvya's search he was introduced to co-author Edna Pasher, a management consultant. Whereas Tuvya was struggling with KM problems on the *tactical* level, Edna was grappling with KM issues on the *strategic* level.

Edna draws from her academic background in organizational communications to guide organizations in strategic renewal processes. Since the 1980s, she has adopted the approach outlined by Hammel and Prahalad,[1] whose focus of strategic processes is to identify the core competencies of an organization that will lead to a sustained competitive advantage. Once these competencies are agreed upon, the question becomes how to develop them in the most effective and efficient way. In order to ensure a sustained competitive advantage, the core competencies—or in other words the core knowledge—should be developed, upgraded, and improved in order to generate a higher return.

Since 1994 Edna has tackled the task of exposing executives to the emerging field of knowledge management. She realized that viewing knowledge as the heart of the competitive edge of organizations implied that knowledge management and strategic management must go hand in hand.

A good example of the power of strategy working in concert with proper KM is IBM Corporation. Its success over the years has relied on a unique combination of technological and business management innovation. IBM allocates billions of dollars of R&D investments to create unique products and adapts them to the changing needs of the market. Further, it develops core competencies in business innovation to influence those market needs. We can see this at work when we think about how IBM was first on the market in creating PC hardware, but then got out of it for more profitable activities later on.

We present a more detailed description of IBM in Chapter 3, but we mention it here as a powerful example of knowledge management and strategic management going hand in hand. In spite of such an obvious model, it is still difficult to persuade managers to take a serious look at strategic KM. The following stories further describe Edna's experiences.

Convincing Managers about the Importance of Strategic KM

When leading strategic processes in organizations, Edna observed that it was very difficult for managers to "think outside the box." It was hard for them to be creative and innovate faster than their competitors. Sometimes managers were better able to incrementally improve what they'd already done rather than to dare to embark on a full paradigm shift.

Edna found that it was extremely difficult to convince managers that knowledge management is a worthwhile pursuit. It is a difficult business case to make because tangible results can take years to come to fruition. Managers of public companies are particularly pressed to show results on a quarterly basis, so they don't often see the results of knowledge management overhaul quickly enough to put the initial effort into perspective.

Even though thinking about strategy at the outset of major tactical changes is a difficult case to make, sometimes Edna is successful, as the following examples show.

Arkia: A Strategic KM Transformation

In the early 1990s, the Israeli domestic airline Arkia was a 40-year-old company, which always did more or less the same thing. It operated domestic flights in Israel and flew short-range international charter flights. The company seemed to be sleepwalking through its processes for many years without change. But when the company managers took a look at their business in terms of strategic KM, a transformation came about.

(continued)

They used the tactical methods of knowledge-creating interactions to gain insight into the experiences of managers and employees. They then arrived at a strategic decision to better exploit existing core competencies. In this particular case, instead of selling vacation packages only on a small scale to accompany flight tickets, they decided to use that capability to make the airline a major tourism company. The result was a major increase in revenues and profits.

The main issues presented in this example are: How to achieve a strategic transformation based on knowledge and core competences (which we detail in Chapter 3)? What are the tactics to produce knowledge creating interactions (which we describe in Chapter 6)?

Danya Cebus: A Construction Company Going Public

Picture this: It is the technology boom of the late 1990s and enthusiastic investors are abandoning the old economy for the lure of high-tech profit. How do you convince potential investors to buy shares in your construction company during a recession in the construction industry?

This was the challenge faced by Danya Cebus, a leading construction company in Israel. Their strategic problem was raising the company's value in a difficult market in preparation for going public. They needed to convince potential investors that they had the possibility for future growth and were just a high-tech company in an old-tech industry. With this in mind, they asked themselves, how does Danya Cebus present its core competencies and demonstrate that it can ensure a sustained competitive advantage in a fast-changing industry?

Although a construction company technically belongs to the old economy, knowledge management turns out to be a relevant tool for addressing their strategic question. They faced the task of presenting their strategic advantage by tallying their knowledge assets and knowledge management practices. Their solutions to staying competitive are presented in Chapter 9. The changes led to successful results.

Holon, Israel: A City Reborn

Cities need to move to knowledge-based development, too, just as organizations do. The city of Holon in Israel had to reinvent itself as it became less attractive to future generations of Israeli citizens. In 1993, a new mayor and CEO started a well-documented renaissance process in the city and the story has become an example recognized worldwide.

The city managers started with a singular vision: Make Holon "The Children's City," thus making it attractive to young families again so they would want to stay there. This strategic focus was then translated into many projects and programs across the area, involving major efforts to turn Holon into an attractive city complete with an intellectual capital (IC) report to visualize all the efforts of the transition.

In 2007, after 15 years of building, the city moved in an Israeli rating[2] from number 15 (last in the rankings of the Top 15 Israeli cities) to number 6. In 2010 its mayor was named one of the world's top 10 mayors by a UK magazine.[3] All it took was a strategic approach from a singular vision. The city's managers followed processes of proper knowledge management toward increasing the city's human capital, thereby enriching its intellectual capital and, in turn, its long-term growth.

These examples demonstrate the broad spectrum of knowledge-based strategies and tactics that apply not only to corporations, but also to many not-for-profit organizations.

A Convergence of Paths

When we (Tuvya and Edna) first met during the late 1990s, our initial discussions produced three conclusions:

1. Tuvya was not alone in searching for tactical solutions.
2. The search for strategic solutions was an even more important step toward proper knowledge management.
3. The search for answers to proper knowledge management is a common journey.

In the rest of this section we elaborate on these conclusions and their significance to our further common work.

Tuvya's Questions Are Typical Tactical KM Issues

Not surprisingly, our first conclusion upon meeting was that Tuvya's knowledge problems were not unique but universal. The problems at Rafael were typical examples of tactical questions in knowledge management:

- How can an organization enhance its knowledge creation?
- How can it preserve its existing knowledge?
- How can it encourage its knowledge sharing?
- What are its most efficient methods of knowledge dissemination?

KM Has Important Strategic Implications

Our second conclusion was motivated by Edna's experience that most managers are initially exposed to KM issues through tactical aspects, but eventually discover that KM has strategic implications that are even more valuable to their long-term goals.

When we met, there were substantial restructurings happening at Rafael. The main change was that Rafael was transitioning from a government organization into a commercial company, in turn emphasizing profitability. Part of the change involved instilling a different system of work contracts. The measures implemented were expected to have positive effects: streamline the organization, decrease operational expenses, and increase efficiency and profits. Then, hopefully, they would lead to better financial results and increase the tangible financial capital of the company.

But the initial expectations should have been further examined from a knowledge management point of view. The changes they were looking for may have led to changes in culture and values, some of which could have influenced worker motivation to create and share knowledge, or even to continue working at the company. In Chapters 4 (regarding culture) and 5 (concerning the human focus), we discuss these kinds of issues and show how Rafael successfully solved them, thus avoiding the need for a second wave of overhaul.

These types of moves for change should raise basic questions regarding identifying the existing knowledge assets of an organization and how to effectively exploit them in a new structure. All these considerations are part of what we call the *intellectual capital* (a term invented in the 1990s—for example, Edvinsson[4] or Stewart[5]—to include all intangible assets that are necessary in the present to assure continuous future success of an organization). Eventually, and fortunately for Rafael, we found that after a decade, the results for Rafael were very successful and carried with them very important lessons. We describe these lessons in Chapter 3 on strategy.

Strategic KM questions that would be helpful for organizations to ask, though, before making sweeping structural changes—questions affecting the intellectual capital of an organization—include the following:

- Are the culture and values at an organization right for a properly knowledge-savvy organization?
- What are the knowledge assets of the organization?
- How can the organization leverage its assets for better results?
- How can it increase its assets in the long run?

These strategic questions are always important overall, but they are even more sensitive in times of turnover and restructuring. Actions leading to short-term gains in financial capital may induce major losses in intellectual capital in the long run if questions like these are not considered. These losses will eventually hamper financial results over time if managers do not take them into consideration as early as possible.

We Would Like to Join Forces in Search of Answers

Our third conclusion upon meeting was that KM questions, both tactical and strategic, are vital to the future success and sustainability of any organization. Hence we want to join forces and embark on a common journey to search for answers.

Discovering Universal KM Truths

We began this journey to discover how KM questions are answered around the world. It began as an actual journey of several months, visiting organizations and consultants who were leaders in KM globally at the time. Our journey then continued as a more comprehensive study of what is actually done, both worldwide and in our home of Israel and especially at Rafael. Our travels have lasted more than a decade, covering ups and downs in the economy (including two economic crises, or so-called bubble economies) and in all types of organizations. Now we would like to share with you the lessons of our journey, beginning with some of the basic answers to some of the basic questions.

The Answers Are Important

We have found that knowledge management solutions always have benefits for an organization. With this in mind, the reader should realize that KM has not yet become a mature discipline. While many organizations are doing well with KM initiatives and processes, there are many others that still need to improve. So it is not enough that people, teams, and organizations are aware of KM issues and solutions. We still need to broaden the various methods involving KM and make its practice even more widespread.

As we've said, in the years since our research began, we have witnessed two economic crises that put KM to the test. The first was in the early 2000s: the technology bubble crisis (or dot-com crisis) in what is now called the new economy or the knowledge economy. Many high-tech companies collapsed at that time, shattering with them many investor hopes and raising doubts about the validity of claims concerning the worth of knowledge-based organizations. This might have led to a misconception that the knowledge economy was finished, but time has proved the opposite. It is true that in the days of the inflated bubble economy, it was difficult to distinguish which companies had genuine intellectual capital and which ones were just claiming to have it. The ones with real IC and effective knowledge management survived and prospered. (In particular, we looked very closely at our home economy in Israel as a good laboratory in which to review case studies of both of these bubble economies, because of Israel's small-scale economy but large-scale start-up culture, and found this to be a common thread.[6])

The second economic crisis occurred in 2008 and has not yet ended. Unlike in the first crisis, knowledge management practices were not to blame in the second. Instead, most professionals agree, the second crisis was more the result of gross financial blunders combined with greed and fraud. However, of the organizations and regulators that have made a comeback and survived since 2008, it's obvious the ones with a better understanding of their organization's knowledge management processes—and better IC—were quicker to rebound than the competition.

These two bubble economies were a magnifying glass with which we could watch the delicate relations between knowledge organizations (KOs) and their knowledge workers (KWs) as they reacted to pressure-filled situations. Because human capital (which creates intellectual capital) is so important to proper knowledge management and, in turn, long-term growth, we dedicate several sections in this book to analyzing the issues of an organization's culture and its human resources.

The Answers Are Diverse

Overall, our quest for the best practices in knowledge management was motivated by both tactical and strategic issues, and the answers we found covered a wide spectrum of the life of an organization: from understanding business models and creating the right culture to human resources and reviewing day-to-day operations of knowledge creation and capturing. Developing a successful system of knowledge management requires a manager to pay attention to every step in the process of an organization's work.

However, because there are so many steps in the process, we tried to stay focused and limit ourselves to the issues most directly relevant to proper knowledge management, including culture, interactions, customers, and innovation. Nevertheless, keep in mind that KM still covers many more aspects than are covered in this book.

We also found that for each aspect we do cover, there is a great diversity of methods for successfully moving toward effective knowledge management. We aim to present the diversity of these methods with as broad a perspective as possible from what we learned worldwide and at home.

Some Answers Can Be Found Close to Home

Another answer we came to was that there was much to learn from organizations near our home. Tuvya, for example, was impressed by what he saw when he visited successful knowledge-managing organizations around the globe, but also learned to appreciate the ways that his own organization does KM: Rafael had been managing knowledge throughout the years, sometimes without even knowing that's what they were doing.

As is the case with many organizations, the founding fathers of Rafael and its workers didn't start out using the term *knowledge management*. They simply knew they needed an excellent R&D organization in order to prosper, and fortunately they succeeded in creating the basics of a knowledge culture—even without knowing that was what they were creating. They adapted their business to changes in the environment over the years, so the culture at Rafael came to consist of many important ingredients that can be used as an example for other organizations.

Expanding this example to our home country, Israel, there is also much to be learned. Israel, a country with no natural resources, must rely on its intellectual capital to survive. This IC is manifested in a start-up spirit that has been documented in literature[7] and through some important KM practices in Israeli organizations. We therefore feel that Israel, and Rafael especially, have a lot to offer as case studies in this book, and we mention them throughout.

While we are boasting of our home, we are sure that your own home organization has some good KM practices, too. While you are probably looking to make KM improvements in your organization, it is also important to notice and understand what you already have. It is a good basis for implementing changes so you do not inadvertently spoil what successful KM practices you already have while you make improvements.

The Manager Must Lead

We hope you keep in mind that knowledge management is the concern of *every* manager. It is not some side issue that may be left solely to chief knowledge officers and management consultants. Knowledge is the most important asset of a modern organization. Only continuous growth of knowledge ensures long-term growth of profit and the tangible capital of an organization. The manager, at all levels of an organization, must be the leader and catalyst of knowledge management. It is the manager who must comprehend the strategic significance of knowledge, instill the culture and processes of creating and sharing knowledge, and, in particular, continually foster innovation (the creation of new knowledge).

This is where you, the reader, come in. Most likely you already know something about knowledge management but are curious to learn more. Many of the problems we describe and address in this book will be familiar to you. We hope to provide you with insight by presenting the methods used by cutting-edge knowledge-managing organizations and to convince you of the importance of proper knowledge management in ensuring the success of your organization. We also wish to provide you with the tools and the plan to implement the proper cultural environment for enhancing the creation and sharing of knowledge within your organization.

Conclusion

This chapter has exposed you to some of the challenges of tactical and strategic knowledge management issues. We have given you some initial answers to a few basic problems and will now continue to lead you on a KM journey by delving into the details. In Chapter 2, we discuss the business reasons for putting time and energy into increasing intellectual capital, the ultimate goal of proper knowledge management.

The Magnificent 7

1. Knowledge is the most important asset of a modern organization.
2. Knowledge management has many important tactical issues, and most managers are initially exposed to KM through these aspects.
3. Knowledge management has strong strategic implications on the organization, and the tactics should be derived from them.

4. Knowledge management is relevant for all types of organizations: small and large businesses, all types of industries, and not-for-profit organizations.
5. Knowledge management should be led by managers at all levels of an organization.
6. There are many diverse methods for knowledge management. Organizations can learn from each other, beginning by realizing what already exists in their own home.
7. Knowledge management is a constant process, whereby processes of creating, sharing, and capturing knowledge should be continually repeated and refreshed.

Making the Business Case for Managing Intellectual Capital

Wisdom exists only in those things that are hidden from the eye.
> —Jewish proverb, circa third century

Anything essential is invisible to the eyes.
> —Antoine de Saint-Exupéry, *The Little Prince* (1940)

In this chapter you will:

Learn about intellectual capital and its importance to managers in the form of valuing intangible assets.

Understand why increasing and managing intellectual capital is essential for the long-term prosperity of knowledge organizations.

Understand why knowledge management is first and foremost about managing and increasing intellectual capital, and how it serves as the basis for all knowledge management tools.

While you may assume so far that knowledge management is important, you still have to convince yourself and your managers about its tangible contribution to your business. You will grapple with questions like, "Intellectual capital is an intangible asset and does not appear in the conventional financial reports, so why bother with it?" This chapter helps to build the business case for investing your time and money into the proper knowledge management systems.

Intellectual Capital as the Basic Asset of a Knowledge-Intensive Business

We have already mentioned that intellectual capital (IC) is the most basic asset of the knowledge organization, essential for ensuring the sustainable success of an organization and continuous growth of its tangible financial capital.

The concept is not immediately understood, so instead of honing our definitions, we will explain it by using several examples from different industries.

Example: AFS, a Skandia Subsidiary—A Company in the Red Gets a Green Light

In the 1990s, Skandia was a leading insurance and financial services company in Scandinavia. However, it was deliberating about the fate of AFS, one of its less successful subsidiaries. Leif Edvinsson, who served as vice president of intellectual capital at Skandia, discussed the situation in an interview[1] he gave in 1997 at Skandia Headquarters:

Skandia AFS in 1990s

Skandia's top managers gathered in Stockholm in the early 1990s to determine the fate of AFS because the company was losing money. At the time, the managers decided to liquidate the company.

But Mr. Edvinsson had been gathering information that painted an altogether different picture from the gloomy financial reports the managers were referencing. In fact, his keen observations of the fledgling subsidiary in the months prior to the meeting had left him optimistic about its ability to succeed in the near future, in spite of its financial losses. Everything he was looking at indicated that something good was happening at AFS that the numbers didn't report—that AFS had what it took to be successful.

Mr. Edvinsson claimed that AFS was making a number of business decisions that would eventually improve its financials. They included:

- Recruiting talented employees.
- Working on developing a sound, long-term business strategy.
- Rapidly increasing its customer base.
- Improving its work processes.
- Implementing extensive information technology capabilities.

At the time, Mr. Edvinsson's analysis convinced Skandia's board that although AFS was temporarily losing in financial terms, it had all the building blocks of a solid company and was moving toward becoming profitable. These crucial building blocks, Mr. Edvinsson argued, were worth further investment, *even at the expense of a temporarily less attractive balance sheet.* The building blocks he described consisted of the type of intellectual capital that enables future growth in spite of a temporary lack in financial capital.

After reviewing the intellectual capital that AFS possessed, the board was convinced to give AFS another chance. The decision proved wise: Within two years the company had indeed become profitable and growing.

Example: An Israeli Machinery Firm—A Company in the Green Gets a Red Light

Around the same time period, in a warmer part of the world, we found a similar story but in an opposite situation. It was described in a 1997 report from the Israeli state comptroller:[2]

The Israeli Machinery Firm

The comptroller's report described the results of auditing a particular government-owned company* specializing in machinery. Its financials were seemingly balanced, but further review showed that its managers had really just focused their cash on showing short-term profits and had invested almost nothing in research and development (R&D).

When the state comptroller reviewed the company's case, they realized that the company's products were outdated and the demand for them was on the decline. Although the financials were sound at the time of the review, without the forward thinking on R&D, the company's reports would soon tell a different story. The comptroller asked the company, "Without R&D, what are you going to sell in a year or two?"

———————
*Not Rafael.

The state comptroller did not use the term *intellectual capital* while doing his review and probably did not even know about the term at that time. But he was able to predict that without renewing its knowledge—and fast—the machinery company would not be able to survive. While some might argue that a state comptroller always tends to predict gloomy results as a part of the job, he was actually right this time. Within a few years, the company in question found itself losing money in spite of receiving an excess of government assistance and eventually was under consideration for liquidation.

In our terms, this company was losing its intellectual capital. Not putting money into R&D means losing structural capital and, eventually, losing human capital because various people within the company, including in R&D, will probably end up leaving.

Example: Tnuva—Apax Invests in IC in a Traditional Industry

More than 10 years later, we discovered another perspective on intellectual capital from a surprising source—Tnuva, an Israeli industry giant in the traditional sense. Established 85 years ago, Tnuva is a food company specializing in dairy products with sales of about $2 billion a year. With over 6,000 employees, Tnuva is a household brand name in Israel (especially for Tuvya, whose father worked for the company for 30 years). But because Tnuva's ownership system was out of date (owned by a cooperative of about 1,000 farmers which generally yielded low profits), it is not a company we would typically look to as an example of being innovative in knowledge management or rich with intellectual capital.

However, the purchase of Tnuva by Apax (an international private equity firm) in 2007 brought about major changes at the company with important implications regarding KM and IC. Zehavit Cohen,[3] the new chairperson of the board appointed by Apax, delivered interesting insights on Tnuva's case in a lecture at a leadership conference recently. Ms. Cohen described several aspects of the turnover in Tnuva following the acquisition, some of which we've included here:

> . . . *Apax does not buy firms for immediate results, like immediate sale for higher price or for ripping cash. We buy firms with high unrealized potential, for which our management team has an added value. So we can upgrade them for a profitable sale in five to seven years . . . .*

> *We were appointing better managers where necessary, but were striving to retain other key personnel . . . .*

> *Our first steps in the turnover of Tnuva included a thorough investigation of work processes, from the top management procedure to the last machine in the manufacturing line. We were working to improve them as fast and as better as possible . . . . This is the way to achieve quick gains . . . .*

You have probably noticed that all the insights Ms. Cohen presented have to do with realizing the intellectual capital at Tnuva upon acquisition.

The components she discussed included both the human and structural aspects of the organization. And if you are not yet convinced that Apax was deeply cognizant of Tnuva's rich intellectual capital and potential for the future, this last quote from Ms. Cohen's lecture may finally prove our point:

> *We started long-term projects for improvement, including investments in processes and equipment. When the economic environment in 2009 hampered some of our financial results, some managers suggested suspending or cancelling these investments. I answered that as we are not a public company, I do not worry about quarterly results in the stock market. We are here to stay for several years, and I need these investments to have better results then. And I am telling you [this] from the point of view of a career CFO.*

Again, she never used the term *intellectual capital.* However, it is obvious that she was outlining how Apax was involved extensively in recognizing IC in its acquisitions and raising its visibility to ensure a better future for its organizations.

A Quantitative Definition of Intellectual Capital

The three prior examples detail how businesses from a variety of industries all understand that financial results are not the only factor in determining the future success of an organization. They take into account other important factors, such as:

- The skill and expertise of a company's human resources.
- The extent and financing of its R&D investments.
- The efficiency of existing and potential work processes.
- A company's IT infrastructure and customer base.

Successful organizations invest in these things even though they are not as tangible as some tactical plans and projects.

The sum of these major factors, and so many more, is what we are calling intellectual capital. While these three examples were picked at random, they represent the fact that most businesses actually do make a point these days to pay attention to intellectual capital.

Professor Baruch Lev, from New York University Stern School of Business, has systematically researched the value of intellectual capital during his career. Professor Lev is the director of the Vincent C. Ross Institute of Accounting Research and the Philip Bardes professor of accounting and finance at that university. The results of some of his research published in 2004 in the *Harvard Business Review*,[4] and of others he cites there, are very supportive of the actions described in the preceding cases. For example, Professor Lev states that, "In the 1990s, U.S. corporations invested about $1 trillion a year on intangibles, similar to what they spent on physical assets."

A trillion dollars is a lot of money, collectively (even though you may feel skeptical after hearing trillions of dollars was poured into the U.S. economy in the 1990s prior to the major economic crises in 2000 and then again in 2008). As a manager, or part of a team of managers in a company, you may try to use this impressive number to justify expenditures on intangible assets like IC that match what you spend on physical assets.

However, if you want to be rigorous, how do you find out if the investment in intangibles is worthwhile? Calculating the value is complicated, as we will explain later. However, Professor Lev gives an estimate of the return on investment (ROI) from investing in research and development (R&D), which is just one component of IC:

> *The annual ROI on R&D investment at that time was in the range of 25 to 30 percent. This is substantially above the returns on physical assets and, just as telling, above firms' cost of capital, even after accounting for the relatively high risk of R&D.*[5]

The research does not lie. And hopefully you are doing the same thing in your business, namely investing in intangibles in addition to physical assets. Even if you aren't entirely familiar with the term *intellectual capital*, you have definitely invested in some of its components throughout your experience, and you may have done it intuitively.

Next, we will help to further establish the value of intellectual capital to a business, and deliver a more systematic method to describe and manage it.

A (Very) Simplified Estimation

The value of intellectual capital, being intangible, is difficult to estimate. Even though the concept was introduced about 20 years ago, it has not yet been incorporated into the formal accounting methods of companies (at least until most recently, beginning in 2010). We nevertheless would like to present some methods you can use for estimating the value of intellectual capital. These methods will help you understand IC, its relation to its components, and its monetary value.

A very simplified estimation of the value of the IC of a company is based on the difference between its stock market value (MV) and its classical book value (BV):

Intellectual capital (IC) = Market value (MV) − Book value (BV)

The classic definitions of the book value of a company are based on financial indicators measuring tangible assets: money, real estate, machinery, equipment, and so forth. Generations of accountants have toiled over perfecting the definitions of these assets, yielding a financial reporting system that reflects the book value.

However, the BV does not take into account any intangible assets. Most of them, like training or process improvement, are not reported. Additionally, R&D investments, which are reported, are considered an expenditure that decreases the BV (even when someone who invests in R&D expects that eventually, in the long run, it will raise the BV!).

The stock market, however, should appreciate the contribution of the intangible assets of the company. The market value takes them into account as indicators of future continuous success, which is what the stock market cares about. For example, if the track record of a company over time shows that it uses its R&D wisely to produce continuous extra earnings, investors may pay higher MV for it.

As demonstrated in Figure 2.1, we see trends in the relations between IC, MV, and BV. For traditional, industrial-type companies, we see that their value consists mainly of tangible assets, and therefore their BV reflects most of the market value of the company according to the stock market. Note, however, that the best of these traditional companies do have some IC

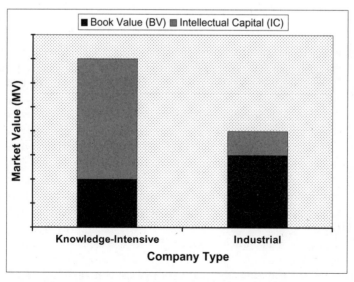

FIGURE 2.1 Market Value and Book Value for Various Company Types

even if it's not recognized as the modern definition of IC, as we saw in the three examples previously mentioned.

And for the more modern, knowledge-intensive companies, we see that the classic definitions of BV are insufficient, and their actual market value (MV) is often much higher than the BV. This gap was observed long before the bubble economy periods of inflated expectations. Annie Brooking,[6] a consultant and author, reported that in the United Kingdom this gap was about 50 percent in 1987; in the United States in the mid-1990s (again, before the bubble crises) it could be anywhere from four to eight times larger.[7]

Take, for example, a typical software company. In the early stages of its life, it does not have or need many tangible assets. Yet, if the stock market appreciates its potential in terms of the quality of its employees and its demonstrated capability to release successful products, it will have a high market value. The intangible assets of IC constitute a major part of its market value. In later stages, this IC should materialize in financial gains and a higher BV. But, to continue to be successful and yield higher earnings, such a company needs continual investment in IC, and those investments will always be a major percentage of its MV.

THE LIMITATIONS OF THE SIMPLIFIED ESTIMATION   While this simplified estimation of IC is useful in helping to explain the concept, we need something more to help estimate its actual value.

The first problem in accurately demonstrating the value of IC is that most readers are now cynics, having lived through two major economic bubbles over the past 10 years, and are probably very suspicious of both MV and BV:

▪ Inflated MV became a major suspect after the popping of the first economic bubble, the high-tech bubble of the early 2000s. At the end of the 1990s, and until the crash in the early 2000s, many companies were traded at a market value that was excessively higher than their book value, sometimes tens and hundreds of times higher. These exaggerated ratios were the result of overly optimistic forecasts about the companies' potential future growth and earnings. The gap, which ultimately proved false, led many people to invest large amounts of money and then ultimately lose it.

▪ Book value got its bad publicity in the second economic bubble, the credit crisis of 2008–2009, when too many firms proved to have fraudulent financial reports.

Obviously, if you believe neither MV nor BV, no one will convince you to believe in IC.

The second problem is that even for mature companies, with an honest BV, it is difficult to have an accurate and proven record of MV for some years. Market value is always fluctuating due to exogenous problems or various investor expectations, and it is generally difficult to use it as a basis for value estimation. In any case, the lessons of the bubble economies are discussed in more detail at the end of this chapter. The following section addresses the value of IC without using MV.

Baruch Lev's Method

Professor Baruch Lev overcomes both of these problems of simplified estimation by introducing a method using actual earnings independent of MV.[8] He looks at the annual earnings of a company, estimates what part of them is due to the customary yield on physical assets in that industry, and assumes the rest is the contribution of the intangible assets. The actual calculations are more complicated (please refer to Lev's original paper, if interested), but they eventually lead to an estimation of the IC of a company. There are some limitations, of course, that prevent Lev's method from becoming part of a formal accounting procedure, but it does give us the ability to quantitatively estimate the dollar value of IC.

A typical example of the IC of various major U.S. corporations according to Professor Lev is given in Figure 2.2.

Here are two immediate observations we can infer from the figure:

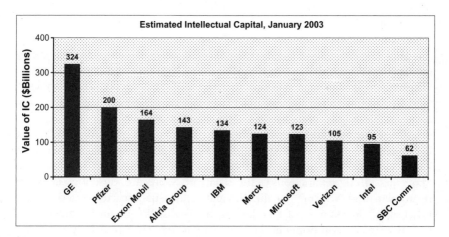

FIGURE 2.2 Example of the Value of Intellectual Capital for Various Corporations
Source: Adapted from data from Baruch Lev, "Sharpening the Intangibles Edge," *Harvard Business Review*, June 2004.[9]

1. The sums are enormous. The IC value amounts into the tens and hundreds of billions of dollars for these corporations.
2. While huge IC expenditures may not be surprising for high-tech giants like Microsoft and Intel, they are also very large for old industries like Exxon (oil) or Altria (cigarettes and food).

These examples highlight that in order for knowledge organizations (KOs) to compete, *they need to increase their intellectual capital.* In fact, that's what knowledge management is all about: increasing IC capabilities. Further, the *primary mission* of any manager is to ensure the organization's long-term prosperity by increasing IC. In order to raise intellectual capital, one needs a systematic method for managing it, as we present in the next section.

In any case, successful firms, especially companies in the high-tech sectors, but also in traditional industry, are having a huge renaissance in IC and investing a lot of money and manpower in regard to management's attention in order to achieve it. The amount of time and money being put toward IC currently is a quantitative proof in establishing the business case for IC and for knowledge management as a systematic way to increase it.

The Systematic Management of IC

If, as we argue, IC is the most basic asset of a knowledge-intensive company, then its enhancement and proper management become chief aspirations. Granted, most well-managed companies do control at least some of the components of IC: human resource practices, initiatives for improving work processes, R&D investment decisions, and so on. Your company is probably an example of one.

However, in light of the importance of IC, and its vulnerability to being overshadowed by short-term financial considerations, we need a comprehensive and systematic method to manage it. We need a common language, akin to the traditional accounting method, that allows us to visualize and measure the intellectual capital of the organization.

There are several known methods to achieve this goal. All of them use the organizational strategy of defining various indicators representing the various components of IC, and presenting them in some structured way. Many are based on variations of the Balanced Scorecard, described in books by Kaplan and Norton,[10] or the Navigator, a visual structure used by Leif Edvinsson[11] in Skandia of Sweden in the 1990s. We begin by dividing IC into two major components: human capital and structural capital (please see Figure 2.3).

Human capital has to do with the people of the organization: their knowledge, innovation capabilities, and skills. Increasing human capital is

Intellectual Capital (IC) =

Human Capital		**Structural Capital**
(knowledge and skills of the individual employees)	**+**	(organizational capabilities that support the employees' productivity)

FIGURE 2.3 Human Capital and Structural Capital

about hiring the right workers and investing (and reinvesting) in their continual training and education. It is an extremely important aspect of a knowledge organization and the focus of numerous knowledge management techniques, as we discuss further in Chapter 5.

The major issue with human capital is that it is not the sole property of the company. It goes home after work and is free to leave the company at any time. Structural capital, by contrast, is an asset that is owned by the company. It is the sum of the organization's capabilities and core competencies. Examples of structural capital include work processes that enable the efficient design of software products, the experience gained in previous projects, investments in R&D, a company's customer base, and so on. We continue to discuss structural capital extensively in most of the following chapters.

The Skandia Navigator

We can present the various components of both human capital and structural capital using the Navigator. The process surrounding the Navigator, developed by Leif Edvinsson in the mid-1990s, is outlined in Figure 2.4.

The process consists of a house-like shape comprising the various components of the financial and intellectual capital of a company. Each component contains various indicators (usually company-specific and not stand-alone numbers) representing its characteristics. The indicators are usually compared to the data of previous years or to what the company has planned or budgeted.

Mr. Edvinsson uses the house as a metaphor for the organization, and its components represent the important building blocks of its capital.

PAST PERFORMANCE   The roof, or attic, is the Financial Focus. Its indicators are usually the standard data in the conventional balance sheet—sales, expenditures, profits, cash flow, and so on. While it is the top result we want to achieve, it actually represents what we have done in the past.

PRESENT STATUS   The main building is composed of indicators pointing to the present activities of the firm. The Human Focus is positioned in the center on purpose, in order to highlight its importance and connection to every other activity: It is the heart of an organization. Typical indicators

FIGURE 2.4 Skandia Navigator—General View

Source: Adapted from Leif Edvinsson[11] and Skandia annual reports 1996, 1997.

are number of employees, percentage with higher education, retention rate, and so on.

The two side walls are the Process Focus and the Customer Focus. Process Focus is a major part of structural capital and includes indicators representing the efficiency of work processes. It may include the cost and/ or time required to manufacture typical products at the company, or indicators about reusing existing knowledge.

Customer Focus includes indicators representing customer base and customer relations, such as number of customers, market share, new or returning customers, results of satisfaction surveys, and so on.

FUTURE RESULTS The basis on which the metaphorical house stands is the Renewal and Development focus, which is directly related to the expected future results. Typical indicators may be the R&D expenditures of a company or its number of new products.

Note that only the first focus area, the financial focus, reflects the traditional book value of the firm. All the other focus areas compose the IC of the company.

Figure 2.5 represents the Navigator with some typical indicators.

A typical manager will concentrate on a small number of chosen indicators, perhaps 10 to 30 covering all focus areas. This may be handled by one spreadsheet. A corporate manager may also need only these indicators, but they will be the aggregate of the various departments. Skandia, which

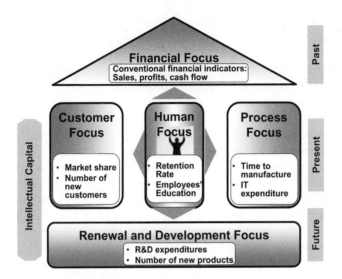

FIGURE 2.5 Skandia Navigator—View with Typical Indicators
Source: Adapted from data from Leif Edvinsson[12] and Skandia annual reports 1996, 1997.

used the Navigator for day-to-day management,[13] used an IT system to handle this process.

The main challenge is not the accounting of the indicators, but the strategic choice of actions in the IC exercise and deciding on the appropriate indicators to measure.

Managing IC Using the Navigator

Managers are the ones who navigate the company. The Navigator is just a tool to assist them. It forces a clear definition of their IC goals and enables them to visualize and measure them.

Take, for example, an investment decision that responsible managers face every year: how much, and where, to spend on R&D and other activities. Baruch Lev describes the outcome of such decisions in the following example:[14]

Example: DuPont's R&D Results

DuPont's textiles and interiors division has more $12 billion in annual sales, and obviously spends considerable resources on R&D. Professor

(continued)

Lev calculated the results of these investments over a period of 15 years from 1985 to 2000:

- *Product R&D,* aimed toward new or improved products, created a value of hundreds of millions of dollars but with ROI not much more than the cost of capital. This is what we usually associate with R&D focus.
- *Brand enhancement activities,* which we usually associate with customer focus, created half the value associated with new and improved products with less investment.
- *Process R&D,* enhancing the efficiency of chemical production processes, created savings worth twice the value of product R&D. These efforts are associated with both R&D and process focus.

Professor Lev's results not only reemphasize the business case for IC, but also demonstrate the possible contribution of its various elements. Not surprisingly, the indicators we gave in Figure 2.5 as examples may be used to track some of the relevant activities described in this DuPont story: R&D expenditures, number of new products, and cost/time to manufacture, among other things

The manager must decide about the direction of the IC process and allocate resources in advance. As we see in the DuPont example, these are major strategic issues. The Navigator cannot make these decisions, nor can Professor Lev's calculations, which are made after the fact. The manager makes these decisions according to the vision and strategy of the company using his experience and the available data and analysis at the time. (We discuss more of this process in Chapters 3 and 9.)

But while the Navigator does not make the strategic decisions, it contributes in many other ways. First, by forcing the manager to systematically evaluate the issues, it brings all areas into focus making managers look at long-term investments instead of short-term profits. Additionally, when the manager makes decisions, he can use the appropriate indicators in the Navigator to assign the proper goals and check their progress. Then, later on, the Navigator aligns the efforts of all the stakeholders in the organization toward the preplanned direction. (A detailed description of using the Navigator to measure and manage performance is given in Chapter 9.)

The Balanced Scorecard (BSC)

The Balanced Scorecard is another systematic method to manage IC.[15] Its goals are the same as the Navigator's: forcing the manager and the organization to take care of IC with all intangible components accounted for. It also arrives at a set of chosen indicators, presented in a structured way, and guides the organization in a desired direction.

The structure of BSC uses different terms, but has a purpose similar to that of the Navigator. It arranges indicators into four categories (called *perspectives* in some versions of the BSC):

- Financial.
- Customer.
- Internal processes.
- Innovation and learning.

Even though we are personally more accustomed to using the Navigator to manage IC (and we like its visualization and simplicity), the BSC does have some important advantages. First, as of the publication of this book, BSC is more popular, with many vendors offering books, training, and/or specialized software applications to specific types of organizations. Second, it has systematic ways to help managers come up with indicators derived from strategy.

However, the end results are similar to the Navigator's: The managers make decisions about IC and knowledge management strategy, and the BSC helps them manage it.

Questions for Believers and Nonbelievers

At this point, we hope that you are realizing the importance of IC and its management. We think that a concerted IC plan is essential to an organization's future success. This importance is reflected quantitatively in the research presented by Professor Lev, and others, in the amounts of time and money that businesses have already put into IC management.

However, we still expect readers to be wary of the intangible implications of investing money and efforts in IC. We round out this chapter with answers to some questions we think you might ask.

Question: In our company, we invest in R&D and take good care of our workers. Why should I bother with IC?

Answer: Well-managed organizations nurture their IC even without explicitly using that term (i.e., whether they realize it or not). Responsible managers pay attention not only to the bottom line financially but to all the parameters that determine the future health of the organization simultaneously. Well-informed managers discuss and plan a firm's marketing and customer base, human resources, training, and work processes, as part of their regular duties.

However, focusing on the concept of IC ensures a more systematic and comprehensive implementation and participation of every stakeholder in the organization. When combined with a structured management tool, such as the Navigator, IC management highlights issues no manager can afford to neglect. Focusing on IC forces managers to discuss a vision and plan a strategy. It requires translating the strategy into action in all focus areas, which entails agreeing on relevant indicators and setting goals for them. Focusing on IC also ensures that managers do not forget the indicators during their day-to-day work.

Question: Can IC indicators be translated into a dollar value? If not, how can the indicators predict future success?

Answer: Unfortunately, there is no algorithm that directly translates IC indicators into a dollar value. Tuvya debated similar questions with Leif Edvinsson during his interview at Skandia.[16] Tuvya claimed that the move to publish the Navigator as a supplement to regular financial reporting could lead to the misconception that such an algorithm exists.

Mr. Edvinsson responded that, eventually, careful management of IC turns into dollar value, and that while each indicator by itself may not have a direct implication for long-term success, their combination enables the company to arrive at a better future. The secret is to work on strategy, identify the key success factors for the organization, tailor the indicators accordingly, and manage them.

Question: Could IC management have prevented the first bubble economy in the early 2000s?

Answer: Yes! The first economic bubble, the high-tech bubble, was characterized by many companies being traded at an exaggerated market value—tens and hundreds of times more than their book value. When analyzing these gaps using IC, we argue that investors could have distinguished between gaps in the BV and MV of the companies involved. Most of the companies that collapsed, in spite of promising innovation in technology and plenty of cash, were lacking important aspects of intellectual capital.

For example, many of them did not identify the need to focus on and thereby develop customer capital beyond the present. For others, a comprehensive assessment of their actual R&D competencies or their work processes would probably have revealed they were not mature enough to generate return on the investment. And still others were overly concerned with their R&D processes alone. Perhaps a tool such as the Navigator would have helped them realize the potential held by their technological innovations by presenting them with a more balanced picture of the total assets (real and intangible) they needed to manage long-term.

But how do we distinguish believing in IC from false optimism? The true test of our claim that IC brings results lies in the development of the indicators that distinguish gaps between market value and book value. These indicators reveal whether the gap results from unrealistic expectations or from measurable competencies in a firm, such as its technology, processes, and customers. The indicators should identify which companies are experiencing bubbles and which have valuable IC cultures, nurtured and systematically managed by their managers.

Question: Could IC have prevented the second bubble economy in 2008–2009?

Answer: Unfortunately, no, IC could not have prevented the recent credit crisis. However, it might help us to get out of it.

Wherever and whenever you look at the recent bubble economy of the late 2000s, you find greed and fraud as the basic cause. Governments, banks, corporations, and the public were trying to get (much) more money from their investments than was warranted by the realistic prospects of return or the intellectual capital in those investments.

When market participants ignore the basic conservation laws of physics, nothing can help. But when we investigate how to get out of the crisis, with limited natural and capital resources available, then we naturally revert to recruiting all available knowledge in a system to create stronger management of intellectual capital.

Question: My organization does not exactly fit into either the Navigator or BSC systems in terms of management. How can I manage my company's IC?

Answer: The concept of IC is important and valid for almost every organization, be it a high-tech company or a more traditional one. Of course, the vision, goals, and strategy may differ from one company to another, in turn creating different indicators, but the goal is the same: fostering a successful culture where IC moves the business forward.

Both the Navigator and BSC systems can be easily adapted to various types of organizations. For example, you can substitute certain financial results with the actual bottom line by which you are measured. Or you can substitute customer-based and/or process-based indicators with more relevant terms. But never forget about human resources indicators and a company's need for strong renewal and development plans. (We elaborate on these indicators in Chapter 9 when discussing performance.)

Most important is to adhere to the concept of taking IC into account and managing it properly. Look at all the aspects of the organization relating to IC and not only the bottom line; then decide your strategy, set your goals, and define the appropriate indicators in order to achieve them.

Conclusion

Nourishing intellectual capital and creating the knowledge culture necessary to increase the different aspects of IC are keys to the future success of organizations.

We believe that once managers internalize this message, they realize that knowledge management is about increasing IC and that increasing IC is the most important thing they can do to ensure an organization's long-term prosperity.

This chapter concludes the first and introductory phase of the KM journey, describing the motivation for using KM to increase IC. The rest of this book provides tools for systematically and comprehensively managing intellectual capital from all angles. The next chapter explains how to use KM to accomplish strategic goals, and the benefits of coupling the two.

The Magnificent 7

1. Managers who are traditionally preoccupied with short-term financial results should ensure long-term prosperity by increasing IC. The business case for paying attention to IC is supported by numerous examples of successful companies and quantitative research results.
2. Knowledge management is about identifying and systematically managing the IC of knowledge companies as their most important asset.

3. It is complicated to measure the value of IC. Some insights may be gained by defining intellectual capital quantitatively as the difference between the organization's book value and its market value, and qualitatively as the sum of the knowledge and skills of the individual employees and the organizational capabilities that support employee productivity.

4. More sophisticated methods for measuring IC, like Lev's, prove that successful firms, especially companies in the high-tech sectors, but also in traditional industry, are having a huge renaissance in IC. They invest a lot of money, manpower, and management's attention in order to achieve it.

5. Managing and increasing IC begins with business strategy, from which key success factors can be derived. For each key success factor, several indicators should be defined to manage and measure the performance. We can use one of the available methods, like Skandia Navigator or the Balanced Scorecard, for systematic management of these indicators in order to increase IC.

6. Careful use of IC indicators could have helped to prevent or alleviate some of the consequences of the two economic bubbles of the recent decade.

7. Successful use of the indicators to increase intellectual capital depends on an organizational culture that supports knowledge management and in which the indicators are known and understood. It is the manager's role to foster this culture.

CHAPTER 3

The Importance of Strategy in Knowledge Management

In this chapter you will:

Learn about devising a knowledge management strategy that derives from and supports the overall business strategy.

Learn that a shared organizational strategy (outlining the vision, core values, and core competencies to achieve it) is a prerequisite for solid knowledge management.

Learn that a business strategy should link an organization's competencies with the needs of its environment.

Understand how knowledge management serves the strategic management process, by drawing upon the knowledge of a company's workers, and leads to the attainment of strategic goals.

A well-planned knowledge management system serves the overall business strategy. It also addresses the fact that knowledge management (KM) requires a strategy of its own. Successful knowledge management does not occur through isolated interventions but through a systematic and comprehensive plan that outlines the specific competencies that a company intends to develop. Ultimately, a knowledge strategy should be tailored to the specific needs and characteristics of an organization.

The following example about Arkia details how a company's look at strategic management essentially became a plan for its knowledge management. At all levels, from strategic management to day-to-day problem solving, Arkia was managed with the aim of taking the most advantage of the knowledge available within the organization and putting it toward achieving strategic goals.

Arkia—A Knowledge-Based Strategic Transformation

In the early 1990s, the Israeli domestic airline Arkia operated in two basic areas: domestic flights and international charter flights. During a routine analysis of strengths, weaknesses, opportunities, and threats (SWOT), developers hired by Arkia presented to the managers ways that they could take advantage of additional competencies available inside their company that could increase their business. For example, in order to promote domestic flights to Eilat, Israel's southernmost city and a favorite vacation spot, Arkia began selling vacation packages that included hotel rooms, car rentals, and passes to its recreation sites.

Edna, who was a part of the panel advising Arkia at the time, presented to them a strategic process in which they could make money from knowledge: Multiply their channels and sell tourism products independent of the flights. Utilizing the knowledge it had at its disposal regarding marketing vacation packages, Arkia was able to open a successful chain of travel agencies alongside its successful airline business.

A few years later, Arkia went through this analysis process again and discovered that it could further its prospects by selling its competencies in airplane maintenance to other companies. Slowly, but surely, Arkia developed an organizational culture in which every worker began the day with the question, "What do we know how to do that we haven't sold yet?" In fact, the change in thinking that Edna and various developers had incited at Arkia eventually made it possible for Arkia to become Edna's competition—it began selling a variety of consulting services to domestic airlines in other countries on how best to utilize their knowledge for new business opportunities.

The knowledge management process that Arkia underwent was a natural extension of its strategic process. Today, Arkia has developed a wide range of services that protect it from the risks of a company operating in the volatile tourism industry in Israel. Without looking at the proprietary knowledge particular to the company and using it to open new streams of income, it might not have survived if it had relied on flights alone.

Developing a Business Strategy Based on Core Competencies

In a dynamic business environment a corporate identity cannot be defined solely in terms of a portfolio of products and services. The life of these commodities is getting shorter and shorter. In electronics, for instance, the shelf life of new products is often just a few months. Hamel and Prahalad, in a breakthrough *Harvard Business Review* article in 1988, suggested that a better way to define the identity and competitive edge of a company is by defining its core competencies.[1] In practical terms this means asking: What does the organization need to know in order to be able to develop new products and services better, faster, and more cheaply than its competitors? For Edna this incited a big epiphany, and she immediately began implementing this new concept in her consulting. She started helping organizations identify their competitive core knowledge and direct them in using it to achieve strategic goals.

Core competencies are more sustainable than products and services, yet as the environment gets more and more turbulent they, too, need to be reinvented, and this is exactly what happened in our example at Arkia. Through a carefully designed evolution and reevaluation, the company was transformed from a core competence of selling domestic and international flights to its customers to becoming a tourism company with the ability to consistently offer new products and services to new customers with new needs and tastes.

Once the Arkia managers evaluated their business and the knowledge available to them, their core competencies shone through and could be further developed and exploited. An airline company needs many more competencies in order to become a tourism company. It needs to be able to take care of a tourist all the way from the initial exploration phase of looking for different vacation spots to getting there, where to stay, as well as what to eat, where to go, and what types of entertainment options are available. Once these competencies were well developed and they began to sell them to customers, they instantly created new opportunities to exploit. Any business can deliver a wider range of customized solutions to new customers developed from its core competencies. At Arkia, they recognized an opportunity in expanding into all aspects of tourism—both in and out of Israel—thus growing their market and income exponentially.

What Is at the Core of Strategic Management?

Strategic management is the process that allows organizations to renew. In their daily lives, people in organizations are busy accomplishing their tasks and worrying about the "how" questions:

- How to complete their duties.
- How to meet deadlines, budgets, and customer demands.
- How to satisfy their managers' requests.
- How to manage their teams properly.

And much less time and attention are paid to the "what" or "which" questions:

- What should they do?
- What tasks should receive highest priority?
- Which goals should be pursued and which should be abandoned?
- What are they doing today that isn't as important for the future?

When organizations do pause to ask these questions, though, they are essentially devising a strategic program.

The Goal: Staying Ahead of the Game

The goal of strategic management is to ensure that the organization does not fall asleep—to gauge what has changed in the external environment and devise an appropriate organizational response. The organization must decide how to adapt in order to take advantage of new opportunities and protect itself from new threats. In other words, the organization decides how it will renew itself.

In a world that is quickly changing, the pace of organizational renewal has to be at least as fast as the external pace of events. Accordingly, the strategic management process should also renew itself.

The Process: Managing Knowledge

Knowledge should be managed strategically. Once the core knowledge of an organization has been defined, a strategy for managing it needs to be designed, too. Therefore, the knowledge management strategy outlines a systematic and comprehensive plan for managing knowledge. Knowledge should not be managed ad hoc. Interventions, no matter how clever or sophisticated, are only successful as part of an overall vision of a knowledge-managing organization (or learning organization). Only when you have this vision can you outline its implications.

We have discovered that a good way to explain this relationship between the business strategy and the knowledge strategy is by using the analogy of a school curriculum:

Strategy Example: The School Curriculum Analogy

When developing a school curriculum, first it is necessary to decide what a student needs to know, and only then is it possible to develop an appropriate curriculum. What a school graduate needs to know is a very strategic question. Is science more important than literature? Is math a core competency in a global world or are foreign languages more relevant?

Edna was once invited to speak to an audience of school district management personnel, teachers, and parents on the question of what competencies will be most needed in a future working environment. After researching this question for some weeks, she ended up with two competencies as the most competitive ones for the future: learning competence and English fluency. These led to a clear knowledge management strategy:

- Teach students how to learn.
- Even more importantly, make them love learning since they will have to continue learning nonstop in an ever-changing world that is moving faster and faster.
- Next, teach them English. It is the most global language of academia and business and will enable them to participate successfully in the new global economy.

The same type of process—from business strategy to knowledge management strategy—is needed in companies, too. First decide what the organization needs to know, and then move to designing how to develop that organizational knowledge.

The Failure of KM without Strategy

In the mid-1990s a large Israeli telecommunications company rushed to implement knowledge management methods without a strategic vision. It bought and installed expensive cutting-edge software, but the software remained unused.

Without strategy planning, there was no understanding of the relevance or meaning of the information technology to the customer. The managers did not design a clear answer to what the organization needed to know before rushing to buy knowledge management IT support. They did not research a good answer to the simple question, "What will a smarter organization look like?"

Smart organizations are learning organizations; they first decide what they need to know, and only then do they develop that knowledge.

How KM Serves the Overall Business Strategy

Traditionally, strategic management is about focusing your efforts. One of the biggest challenges in planning strategy is choosing the focus of resources and eliminating secondary options. Although the need for focus in strategic planning remains, there is also a new need: In an uncertain world characterized by frequent changes, organizations need to attune themselves to a wide band of opportunities and threats and maintain flexibility. They can do this by continuously learning and keeping their eyes open to the outside world. Managing knowledge in an organization is about fostering learning processes and being open to external radii.

As we said, product life cycles are getting shorter. Instead of considering the organization's strategy in terms of the ideal mix of products and services, the organization needs to identify the capabilities that provide a sustained competitive advantage. Organizations can learn from individuals in this matter.

When someone is planning her career, she asks herself, "What do I need to learn to ensure a sustained competitive advantage in the job market?" Just as individual careers are becoming more dynamic, with predictions of four to five career shifts for the average adult, organizations will have to forget, or unlearn, some of the competencies that created past profit and develop new competencies for future growth. If an organization is too focused, what will it do when its current sources of strength wear out? The secret of an organization's strategic success lies in becoming an open laboratory for the next generation of exciting ideas in addition to an ongoing production of products that, at least for the time being, are sources of profit.

This approach is a real revolution in strategic management and may imply that there is no common path in strategic planning in such an uncertain and dynamic environment. But one conclusion does emerge: Just as an individual who wants to succeed needs to continuously learn all his life in order to ensure that his knowledge does not become outdated, only learning organizations can ensure their future success. Strategic management is an integral part of a learning organization on both the tactical and strategic levels. Ultimately, the organization's strategy provides an answer to the question, "What should we learn?" And the answer should be as broad as possible.

FINDING VALUE FROM INTANGIBLES   In his book *Value-Driven Intellectual Capital*, Patrick Sullivan claims that intellectual capital (IC) and KM are transformed into a tangible dollar amount in many different ways according to the nature of an organization's activities.[2] He details that when an organization's primary activities focus on creating knowledge and sharing technological breakthroughs, it can take advantage of its activities by translating them into new marketable products and selling patents. Providers of professional services, such as lawyers, accountants, and consultants, sell their human capital directly. Other companies generate value through creating and improving processes that raise profits and sales, improve market share, reduce costs, and improve productivity. By dividing firms into four categories—differentiated products companies, commodity products companies, network services companies, and direct service companies—Sullivan enables each type of firm to identify the kind of value it can and should extract from its intellectual capital.

Successfully Using Employee Knowledge as a Strategic Input

Strategic planning used to be the exclusive task of the CEO, who ultimately was responsible for its outcome, and senior managers, whose responsibilities included long-term planning. Increasingly, however, all levels of an organization are involved in strategic planning. The dynamic organizational environment requires employees at all levels to concern themselves with strategic issues. Middle managers in particular should be trained to incorporate strategic thinking in all of their activities.

The Demand: Evaluating Strengths and Weaknesses

Strategic thinking implies sensitivity to external trends and the ability to detect weak signals of changes in the market, in consumer behavior, in customers' expectations, in competitors' behaviors, the implications of new technologies, and the demand for human resources. Strategic thinking requires developing the courage to look in the mirror and honestly assess your strengths and weaknesses. Strategic thinking also includes collecting information about competitors, maintaining intimate contact with customers—even when they are satisfied—in order to identify opportunities, and continually assessing strengths and weaknesses.

These tasks cannot be left only in the hands of those at the top of the organizational hierarchy. The more the people at all levels of the organization concern themselves with these issues, the higher are the chances for future success.

The Tool: Effective Communication

One of the tools to get people together to share their knowledge is known simply as a *knowledge café*. This is a format for meetings especially designed to promote knowledge creation and sharing. It is a method that involves many people at once in a conversation regarding a particular issue that the management chooses. It can be particularly beneficial when management is making a significant decision and is interested in broad input from various perspectives in the organization.

A description of the format of a knowledge café is given in Chapter 6 regarding encouraging interactions. Another example is also given later in this chapter in the section on IBM. Brainstorming meetings like the ones at IBM can improve the quality of a group's decisions by incorporating multiple perspectives. The extensive involvement of the people taking part in the meetings leads to a widespread commitment to a decision. It also is a relatively short process, lasting anywhere from a couple of hours to a half day, but has significant added value relative to cost.

EXAMPLE OF A KNOWLEDGE CAFÉ: LEARNING IN RETROSPECT AT ARKIA   Recently, in a roundtable conversation on innovation management, Professor Izzy Borovich told the story of the knowledge café he conducted with Edna in Arkia when he became its CEO:[3]

> *When I came from the university to Arkia, I found a 40-year-old company that [did] more or less the same things, and then Edna and I reached a conclusion that we should do something in order not to let the company sleep. If you sleep, you do not innovate and if you do not innovate, you die. We decided that in order to find out what and how to innovate we should listen to the employees and we designed a Knowledge Café.*
>
> *Thanks to the ideas of the employees who know the company best (they are its real sensors), Arkia—an airline—became the biggest tourism company in Israel in that time. Arkia had flown to Eilat for years and used to sell rooms in the local hotels to its flight passengers. It had a contract with the Eilat hotels. In our Knowledge Café, one Arkia mechanic said, "Why should we not sell rooms in hotels in Eilat to those who do not fly with us there, but come in a car?" Somebody else said, "And if we sell rooms in Eilat, why should we not sell hotel rooms in Netanya (another resort town in Israel)?"*
>
> *At the end of the process, we had contracts with all the hotels in Israel and sold exponentially more tourism packages annually, bringing in more revenue than ever before.*

Example: IBM—Ongoing Strategic Renewal

IBM's success over the years relies on a unique strategic combination of technological innovation and innovation in business management.[4] The following paragraphs illustrate the strategy at IBM that makes it a role model. (Innovation is discussed further in Chapter 10, among other places.)

Technological Innovation

In order to achieve success, IBM has always run the largest R&D array in its field, putting the company at the head of the U.S. patent receivers list for the past 17 years in a row. In that context, it is worth mentioning that in 2009, IBM research labs in Israel received over 50 new patents in the United States and took first place in U.S. patents for Israeli companies. A necessary condition for the success of such R&D centers is proper management of its employees, the knowledge workers (KWs). (We discuss the challenges of managing KWs and the methods to respond to them in Chapter 5.)

Along with an annual investment of over $6 billion in R&D, IBM has participated in a methodical process of acquiring companies and technologies particularly in the area of software. Over the past decade, this process has allowed IBM to present the most extensive, complete, and advanced product array available.

Over the years, IBM figured out how to adapt to the changing needs of the markets and has transformed itself accordingly. This transformation, brought about by exploring other fields of development, created a sea change whereby the company's priorities were completed renewed.

Because of its extensive focus on R&D, IBM basically invented the use of personal computers as a business model, and later conceived the world's most familiar mobile computing brand, the Think Pad. In spite of being a pioneer in these products, several years ago IBM made a brave decision to leave the mobile computing and printing markets in order to focus on areas where it realized it could provide a true added value to its clients.

Business Management Innovation

IBM's business agenda and long-term vision have made it what it is today: a company that provides an extensive and complete array of services and solutions including software, hardware, and methodology, as well as providing a deep understanding and knowledge of the various fields to which it provides its services.

IBM innovation is also one of modern business models. In the early days of the Internet, IBM was active as an Internet service provider, constantly creating new paths. Today, IBM is laying the foundation of new data analysis applications such as business analysis and cloud computing.

With bandwidth on one side and a fast-growing technological rate on the other, IBM presents analytic computing as the next generation of its technological vision based on data analysis research that has generated new insights into improving its future business. These areas of activity, such as developing business intelligence and information analysis plans, provide clients with the capabilities to use their information more wisely and to extract new business insights, allowing them to eventually increase profit and competitiveness in a flatter, more mechanized world.

In addition to technological innovations brought about by its R&D, IBM has always initiated internal innovation-accelerating processes such as global brainstorming. Innovation Jam is one such resource and is held periodically on the internal communication network of the company. In this event, tens of thousands of employees, customers, and business partners all get together to share new ideas, conduct debates, and realize new insights regarding future trends, new services, and more. (See Chapter 6 for many other methods of interactions for sharing and creating knowledge.)

And lastly, acquisition and merger strategies brought about by these brainstorming sessions, among other things, have led to IBM's acquiring of global companies that are also bringing innovative capabilities to the mother company in the form of new products and services. Most of these M&A deals serve to complement and complete services, solutions, and products already at home at IBM.

Example: Rafael—A Strategic Transformation

During 2001 Rafael Advanced Defense Systems Ltd. was officially transformed from a government unit into a commercial, government-owned firm. This was the culmination of years of debates and deliberations with both hope and concern from various stakeholders. The end results, however, were very impressive:

- Within a decade, Rafael turned from a heavily subsidized government unit into a highly profitable company in terms of defense industry standards.
- It attained an important positioning in the global market, while keeping its technological leadership focused in Israel.

Relative to this book, we see the lessons in this example at Rafael as relevant to the connection between strategy and KM. In 2009, statistics on Rafael's position appeared in a newspaper article.[5] The data demonstrated the progress Rafael had made in part because of its transformation in 2001:

- Sales doubled from 2004 to 2009: from $800 million to $1600 million.
- Profits grew from almost zero (about $1 million) a decade ago into about $112 million.
- Its workforce grew from 5,000 employees in 2006 to 6,000 employees in 2009. Younger, niche-oriented engineers, technicians, and programmers made up most of the new workforce.

Analyzing the sources of these success factors from a KM perspective, we can credit several strategic decisions that evolved through the years. The backbone of these decisions was to combine the company's traditional core competencies of technological excellence and commitment to Israeli defense with a sharpened, profit-oriented management and style coupled with better marketing capabilities. This is not a trivial combination, as we see in the following details.

- First, Rafael decided to adhere to its core mission as "a significant contributor to the security of the state of Israel."[6] The consequences of this were not the best for profits over the short term, but were essential to maintaining the values of the organization and its workers (see Chapter 4 on culture) and proved profitable over the long term. Rafael added the value of becoming a "growing and profitable" company to its mission, and succeeded in sharpening its business management.
- Further, Rafael decided to continue being a leading innovator in technology and systems. For them, this meant investing heavily in independent R&D[7] and attracting outside funding (see Chapter 10 on innovation).
- Simultaneously, Rafael strove to retain its human capital (knowledge workers, including leading-edge engineering and scientists, and also experienced technicians with relevant skills). During such major changes at a company, managers are usually concerned that KWs may leave. Some lessons from their efforts to retain workers during change are described in Chapters 4 and 5. While maintaining its important KWs, Rafael also succeeded in recruiting younger generations to join its mission. It used its positive knowledge culture (for more on this, please see Chapters 6 and 7 on knowledge capturing and creation) to efficiently transfer the knowledge of older generations to newcomers, and incorporate them into appropriate teams in order to create new knowledge.
- Lastly, Rafael also listened to its customers more effectively and incorporated their needs by using some of the methods described in Chapter 8.

In summary, even though Tuvya began his KM journey to learn about what is done throughout many different kinds of organizations, he was proud to find that his home organization was a leading teacher in using strategy to improve its own knowledge management.

Conclusion

This chapter highlights the benefits of coupling knowledge management with strategic planning and outlines the positive implications of these two activities working in concert. You have learned so far that for successful KM you first need a business strategy, and then you need to derive from it a strategy for KM. Only then can you start implementing all kinds of methods and support systems. The various examples in this chapter helped to highlight some strategic issues and their implications for the knowledge aspects we discuss in the following chapters of the book.

Please note that strategic planning should be the result of an extensive process, though, and is beyond the scope of this chapter. There is, however, an abundance of excellent literature on the topic available to you if you would like to hone those particular skills, too. To this end, we provide a few suggestions of books in the Notes section to this chapter for your convenience.[8]

The next chapter describes the second prerequisite for knowledge management—establishing the proper culture.

The Magnificent 7

1. An organizational strategy—including a vision, mission, and strategic goals—must be determined and shared as a prerequisite to knowledge management.
2. Knowledge management serves the attainment of the overall business strategy.
3. Strategic management planning in a turbulent environment should draw upon the knowledge of all the workers and should be periodically revisited.
4. If an organization does not have appropriate strategies that link its competencies with the needs of its environment, knowledge management will not help. If, however, the organization has successful knowledge management processes, the chances of developing an appropriate corporate strategy increase.
5. Knowledge management requires a strategy of its own.
6. Engagement is a key success factor in strategy development. Experiment with innovative methods such as knowledge cafés to engage as many stakeholders as possible in the strategic planning process.
7. Spend time on strategy creation before rushing to implementation of new ideas. Strategic mistakes are very expensive. Try to avoid them.

CHAPTER 4

The Role of Culture
in a Successful
Knowledge-Creating and
Knowledge-Sharing Organization

In this chapter you will:

Learn that knowledge management hinges on developing a system of shared values and norms, and a management style that seeks employees' knowledge.

Learn that this management style is based on a shared culture, trust rather than hierarchical command and control, and respect for the knowledge of the workers.

Receive guidelines for embarking on the complex process of assessing your culture and changing it to fit with successful knowledge management.

There is a certain desirable organizational culture with positive values and norms which is a prerequisite for knowledge management. To attain the desired culture, it is your duty as a manager to assess the current situation in your organization and make the necessary changes.

Initially we were not sure if the culture issue was so important that it really required a lot of detail. But the unified message we got from managers we've consulted with convinced us it was a key component of a solid knowledge management process:

Why Bother with Culture? A Unanimous Message

A decade ago, when Tuvya began his study on knowledge management (KM), he went on a tour, visiting various organizations in Europe and the United States. Almost every conversation with each local KM expert began with the same mantra: Without the right organizational culture and values, you cannot have proper knowledge management.

His hosts also seemed to be suspiciously in agreement about what the right culture involved:

- Positive company values that are commonly shared by all managers and employees.
- A management culture that seeks an employee's knowledge, and is based on trust rather than hierarchical command and control.

Tuvya was overwhelmed by the intensity and similarity of the message. Again and again these experts emphasized the same basic ideas: that you need to find common, shared, and positive group values among your colleagues; treat people well and empower them; and refrain from intimidation tactics. While these KM experts might have a common (and more liberal) background, the same message was given by various other people, all expected to present a capitalist or "strictly business" viewpoint:

- When Tuvya met a venture capitalist, he opened by saying, "Well, before we begin talking about knowledge management, I must tell you that the most important thing is having the right organizational culture ..." (You can guess the rest.)
- Another "strictly business" example is from Pat Sullivan's book *Value Driven Intellectual Capital.*[1] This book is decidedly about economics and extracting dollar value from intellectual capital. Sullivan nevertheless dedicates a full chapter to the same message, describing the "right culture" and emphasizing its importance.

While Tuvya believed culture was important to an organization, he also thought it was self-evident. He assumed that everyone working with—or in—knowledge organizations would see it as obvious enough to not even mention it in too much detail. So why did participants feel the need to push this point over and over? We think there is a strong message here, which should not be considered obvious or trivial, about the need for the right culture and values, and we dedicate this chapter to that message.

The Definition of Culture

Culture is composed of three building blocks: beliefs, values, and behavioral norms. Values hold a central position in organizational culture. They reflect the person's or the organization's sets of beliefs and assumptions about the external and internal environment. They also serve as the basis of the norms that underlie behavior. These norms, and many of the behaviors associated with them, reflect the organization's values. This is why it is so important to address values in managing knowledge—they relate to both norms and beliefs. They reflect backward, since changing values can change beliefs, and forward, by affecting norms of behavior.

Knowledge management involves instilling certain kinds of values in the organization. These values have at their core a high appreciation and respect for individual knowledge, as well as a commitment toward fostering knowledge interactions through mutual trust. An organizational culture that promotes knowledge management is founded on the perception that everyone stands to gain by sharing and creating knowledge. It is a win-win culture, in which both individuals and the organization benefit. Fostering this kind of culture requires that organizations invest in their knowledge workers (as we discuss in detail in Chapter 5) and that their workers commit to the organization's goals.

In this chapter, we elaborate on the development of the shared values that promote knowledge management. Some of the values, such as trust, respect for the knowledge worker rather than hierarchical command and control, and moral identification with the organization's goals, are universal knowledge management values. This means that no matter the size or type of organization, successful knowledge management requires an organizational culture that is founded on these values.

However, the organization also needs to *customize* its organizational culture and values to promote knowledge management in light of its particular characteristics and history. Obviously, by definition, we cannot dictate what these customized values should be. However we do provide a few guidelines for how you can assess your own organizational culture and the extent to which the values it contains promote knowledge management, and how, in collaboration with your employees, you can develop the kind of organizational culture that optimizes knowledge management.

This chapter rests on the assumption that you, the manager, are responsible for implementing an organizational culture for managing knowledge. Knowledge management practices cannot be implemented in an unsupportive organizational culture. They are doomed to fail. Therefore, developing your organizational culture is a prerequisite for successful knowledge management.

Addressing the Nonbelievers

At this point we might risk losing a large portion of our readers because many managers are cynical and skeptical about the importance of culture. Why? Some think the issue is too abstract so, even if they do agree, they aren't quite sure what to do next. Other opponents may recall real events, as well as perceivable frauds, such as:

- *Enron.* There is always someone who mentions how Enron, the benchmark of company frauds, had one of the best-written ethical codes, and a nice set of declared company values.
- *Monsanto.* A lesser-known story is about the chemical industry giant Monsanto. While being a respectable company, from which we can learn even on KM issues, it has had a problem with the way its values were perceived by some of the public. As their PR campaigns touted their values of "feeding the world" and "sustainable development," they could not dodge the criticisms of the thousands of demonstrators who protested against their "industrialized food" and almost put them out of business.

Others may have become cynical after witnessing various attempts and failures to define company values in their own organization or in others. In such cases, they likely experienced an ill-managed process of defining the values of their organization. Sometimes it consisted of too many long discussions, which produced too few declarations, with too little resemblance to reality and with almost zero future effect on the company.

We sympathize with those who make some of these cynical remarks, because sometimes they are well earned. Nevertheless, we urge the skeptics to continue reading and see whether the process can be improved.

The Moral Aspects of Organizational Culture

The moral foundations of the organization underlie and must be established before the specific values related to KM. We believe that it is important for the values that form the basis of an organization's culture to appeal to workers' moral dimensions. This moral element can recruit their commitment by fostering their identification with the organization's goals. It is therefore an important ingredient for knowledge culture.

We usually think of values as belonging to a higher moral realm, as is the case with values of honesty, equality, and fairness. However, in the organizational context, maximizing profit and crushing competition can be defined as organizational values. In fact, sometimes these two types of values contradict, which may make it difficult to articulate a coherent organizational culture.

We illustrate the issue of moral value and its relevance for KM by presenting two examples from Israel. The first one is about Rafael, a well-established organization which could have lost some of its knowledge workers due to changes in mission:

Example: Rafael's Mission

The original mission at Rafael was developing technology for the protection of the state of Israel. It was founded as a unit of the government around 1948 during the Israel War of Independence. The founding generations felt that their homeland was in a vulnerable position, and decided to contribute their intelligence, training, and efforts toward protecting national safety. Their willingness to help protect their country motivated individuals to work for Rafael, although they could get much more comfortable jobs and more recognition in academia, or earn higher salaries in other private companies.

Beginning in the early 1990s, though, Rafael became increasingly oriented toward an economics-based strategy. New values skewed toward profitability arose, and threatened to dominate the initial values Rafael held as a protector of the nation. As Rafael increasingly sought customers outside of Israel, many workers were concerned that their mission conflicted with their development of solutions to Israel's security needs. Typical employee questions included:

- If profit is the true driver in the company in terms of its business decisions, why shouldn't I also seek a higher salary elsewhere?
- Will we continue to work on innovative, cutting-edge projects, or will we just exploit existing knowledge for higher profit?

This clash of values culminated in 2001 when Rafael was transformed into a government-owned company. Many workers began to feel that the old Rafael values with which they identified no longer existed, and these feelings had implications for the knowledge management aspect of the culture at the company. Without higher organizational values with which to identify, and with the prospect of potentially less interesting projects, Rafael managers faced the risk of losing some of their best knowledge workers.

Fortunately for Rafael, it ultimately succeeded in incorporating both values of caring for national security and profitability in its mission. It is a major player in leading national security projects, based on

(continued)

cutting-edge technologies. Its sales volume and value have increased significantly since 2001, both regarding monetary value and qualitative importance. At the same time, Rafael increased its export—up to about 75 percent of its sales in 2009—which created profits and sources for more R&D.[2]

As business continued from 2001 on, employees saw the company's old values being restored and, at the same time, discovered the benefits of working for a financially stable company. Its profitability does not conflict with caring for national security and developing newer technologies. On the contrary, the two components support each other. In spite of initial concerns of conflict in the company's goals, Rafael retained almost all of its knowledge workers (see Chapter 5 for details) because employees are confident in the company and proud that it has contributed to a safer Israel.

This example may make you think about what type of corporate culture you want to foster at your company.

Our second example details a very different organization: the ad hoc consortium that built the Cross-Israel Highway. Understanding its mission and core values was crucial in mobilizing its workers to contribute to the effort and get the project out of crisis.

Example: The Cross-Israel Highway[3]

Highway 6, the Cross-Israel Highway (named after Yitzhak Rabin) is known to most Israelis as a major success story. The highway was a first in Israel in many terms: length, size, superior quality of construction, and extensive environmental protection. Construction of the highway began during the late 1990s, continued through the early 2000s, and was completed earlier than expected (in about five years). This was achieved in spite of many exterior disturbances, created by various serious political issues. Despite these controversies, in the end, it did make the peripheral towns much closer to the center of Israel. It also was a first in terms of business model because it was a toll highway constructed as a build, operate, and transfer (BOT) project with a value of about $1 billion.

Even though it was a high-profile project in Israel, very few people know the inside story about the organizational problems that the consortium building the highway was facing. It was a joint venture of three companies: two from Israel and one from Canada. The consortium suffered from the conflicting interests of the three partners. Unlike the Rafael example, the consortium workers had no common past legacy and expected no common future after completing the project. The combination of the daunting task set before them, the huge exterior disturbances, and the potential for organizational chaos threatened the whole operation's success.

Edna was hired as an organizational consultant on the project and quickly realized there was actually one simple, common value shared by all parties involved: the dream and vision of seeing this highway built and operating. She presented the idea and persuaded top management to intensify the commonality of this vision by adding even more value: Make the dream happen, but also make it happen "on time, on budget, and on spec."

In the end, they were successful in convincing most employees to believe in these values. Of course, just sharing the common values did not solve all their problems. However, it definitely changed the mood of the project, helped workers to overcome conflicts of interest, and encouraged everyone to contribute their knowledge to make the dream a reality.

The lesson of these two cases can be summed up this way: Working toward common values in which one believes and with which one identifies can be an important source of motivation for workers in a common corporate culture. Overall, knowledge management stands a greater chance of success when it is rooted in positive moral values where workers can identify with an organization's goals. While it seems obvious, this moral element must not be neglected and should be a part of any manager's plans for improving an organization's future.

The Practical Aspects of the Right Organizational Culture

There is a saying among management consultants about the differing interactions between managers and workers in the United States and Israel. It's anonymous, and goes something like this:

In the United States, when a manager just makes a suggestion, his workers consider it a decision;

In Israel, when a manager makes a decision, his workers consider it just as a suggestion . . .

This joke, stereotyping both cultures, demonstrates the dilemmas in defining and implementing the right organizational culture that are discussed in the following section.

Does Your Management Style Seek an Employee's Knowledge?

To utilize an employee's knowledge, you must have a management culture that actually seeks it. Obviously, the culture must be based on trust rather than hierarchical command and control.

Pat Sullivan's book, mentioned at the beginning of this chapter, dedicates a section to the relation between management style and willingness of employees to innovate, create, and share knowledge.[4] Figure 4.1, adapted from his book, shows the evolution of management style from an authoritarian stance to a more open one, and the respective employee response.

Obviously, authoritarian and hierarchical management style is undesirable for any KM culture. Employees will obey orders (grudgingly) and will not contribute their own knowledge. As the style becomes more and more open, employees take more responsibility, creating and innovating new knowledge.

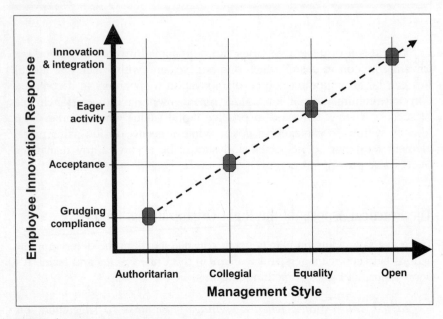

FIGURE 4.1 The Effect of Management Style

Source: Adapted from Patrick Sullivan, *Value-Driven Intellectual Capital: How to Convert Intangible Corporate Assets into Market Value* (New York: John Wiley & Sons, 2000).

While we argue to move out of an authoritarian style of management, we do not advocate a fully open style as the ultimate goal. Usually, some hierarchical control must be exercised, so we will probably choose some style in the middle. Hence, one of the key challenges in customizing a knowledge management culture and a set of values for your organization entails deciding on the extent of freedom that you will grant to individual workers.

The optimal style is therefore customized for every organization overall, and even for each department within that organization. Take Intel, for example. Intel is a company that boasts a free and innovative culture in its research and development departments. But at the same time, Intel uses the restrictive slogan "Copy Exactly" in its worldwide fabrication plants, where changes in its mass-produced chips are frowned upon.[5]

The optimal style may also need to be customized depending on the situation. For example, organizational behavior consultant Dr. Ichak Adizes advocates that every organization should immediately change from democracy to dictatorship when it makes a major decision:[6]

- Employ democracy before you arrive at a decision; in this way you exploit the organization's knowledge by asking every relevant player for input and collecting various opinions.
- Use dictatorship after you have decided; then everyone must follow.

Dr. Adizes' example is obviously an exaggeration of an extreme change of style in a very short time, just to prove the point. More realistic changes are described in the paragraphs that follow.

Organizations may vary in their actual positions with respect to the desired optimal style of communication between a company and its workers. In many cases, the optimal style may also need to be amended depending on the most current situation. Figure 4.2 presents a visual representation of this issue. It shows how the goal of every organization should be to maintain its culture in the medium "optimal" zone by using the management style appropriate to it.

Many knowledge management experts suspect that many companies are still trapped in the bottom zone of this figure, which is too authoritarian and restrictive. This is why everyone Tuvya met on his benchmark visits emphasized the culture issue (as described in the beginning of this chapter). For many companies, this top-down management style was appropriate in the industrial age, but the modern knowledge economy requires making adjustments. Even being at the forefront of modern management techniques does not guarantee that you are in the optimal zone of management style. For example, top management is often more committed than middle management to freer forms, so work still needs to be done on creating a change vector, like curve A shown in Figure 4.2.

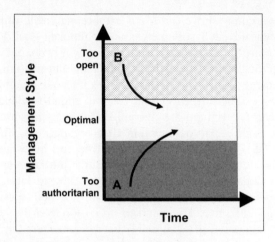

FIGURE 4.2 Management Style—Change Vector in Time

Some organizations actually suffer from the opposite problem. For Tuvya, it was obvious that organizations need the right culture and values but that was because he grew up in an organization (at Rafael) with an open culture and managerial approach. His organization, however, may have been in the top "too open" zone. Some of Rafael's departments were managed like academic institutions, with too much freedom for an organization that is supposed to deliver products. Preaching for a freer style was dangerous for them, and might have driven them even farther from the "optimal" zone.

In recent decades Rafael instituted changes along curve B in Figure 4.2, increasing planning and awareness of business considerations. Most people consider it as a success, because it made Rafael more efficient while retaining many of the good ingredients of the knowledge culture. Others warn against it as an overshot. They claim that their departments are too strict now. In their opinion the change to vector B has gone too far into the bottom "authoritarian" zone, and Rafael needs to loosen up a bit.

In summary, the right culture and values are relative, and should be customized to the specific needs and situation of each organization. You need to define what the right zone is for your organization, and assess where you are with respect to the desired zone, then take the required steps for a change.

Do You Encourage Knowledge Sharing?

The willingness to share one's knowledge is obviously a necessary condition for successful KM. But why would employees not keep information to themselves about what they do? The answer has many implications, as we detail in the following example about BP Amoco.

EXAMPLE: THE KNOWLEDGE-SHARING CULTURE AT BP AMOCO A leading example of a positive knowledge-sharing culture is BP Amoco, an energy company with over 100,000 employees. It is a company that successfully instilled a knowledge-sharing culture, one that helped it to survive two mergers in recent years. *[Please note: At the time of this writing, the disaster from the April 2010 oil crisis in the Gulf of Mexico was just beginning, so while we know this company is now facing major issues, this example is still a positive one specifically regarding the opportunities a knowledge-sharing culture can bring to its employees.]*

In the 1990s, BP Amoco established peer groups in which leaders from different business units met to discuss common challenges and how they faced them.[7] The peer groups were initiated by John Brown, who was then a division head and, since 1995, had also been CEO. With time, the groups increased their added value by focusing on results, not only sharing knowledge for their own sake. The groups assumed responsibility for allocating capital resources among business units in the group and for setting unit performance targets.

In general, business unit managers at BP Amoco have a two-part job description. The first part has to do with managing their independent profit-loss units according to traditional business and managerial performance criteria. The second part has to do with engaging in a variety of cross-unit knowledge-sharing activities that are expected to consume between 15 to 20 percent of their time. As described by Hansen and von Oetinger,[8] this system creates "an open market of ideas," whereby people know where expertise lies and feel free to get help directly from the relevant sources. In a knowledge-sharing culture, managers do not have to go through headquarters when they face a problem; they can seek assistance from their peers and be sure that they will receive the information they seek.

BP Amoco managed to successfully instill an organizational value for its employees, one that is the foundation of many behavioral norms and practices of successful knowledge-managing companies: knowledge sharing. Most smart people want to be recognized for their intellectual capital. Therefore, they possess a natural need to share their knowledge. In fact, often it is the organization that prevents knowledge sharing, not individuals. Just as the organization can stifle knowledge sharing, it can also enhance it, as in this case at BP Amoco.

EXAMPLE: THE KNOWLEDGE-SHARING CULTURE AT RAFAEL   Another example of a knowledge-sharing culture is at Rafael, and its story seems too good to be true.

Rafael is blessed with a knowledge-sharing culture. People are usually happy to share their knowledge, whether with new workers, colleagues, or managers. Knowledge sharing is widely practiced throughout the whole organization. There are some isolated islands where people do not share knowledge, but they are just exceptions to the rule. In Tuvya's various encounters with workers, they almost always voluntarily praise this facet of Rafael. It is a heritage that has survived decades of transitions there.

While Rafael is probably not the only company with such a culture, it is quite unique. In most high-tech industries and start-ups, people do collaborate but many times keep some information to themselves as a power source. We got accustomed to the knowledge-sharing behavior at Rafael but we cannot claim that we have done something intentionally to promote it—it just works. Obviously, managers and employees there have been doing something right for many years. It is something we had better understand in order not to spoil it.

But what is it, exactly? There are several possible answers which work together to become effective:

1. Employees have a tenured working contract, so people are not afraid of losing their position of power.
2. Workers share common moral values.
3. There is a positive management style employed throughout the company and its levels.

Overall, the best answer as to why Rafael's culture is so positive is probably a combination of these answers. Also, the old, semi-academic management style of the original Rafael culture, though not really in practice any longer, contributed to a heritage of knowledge sharing—a heritage passed down from generation to generation of workers. But we cannot know the precise combination that makes this positive culture thrive, as many other organizations with similar characteristics to Rafael did not achieve the same results. At Rafael, the knowledge-sharing culture has definitely become a part of its genetic code.

From a managerial standpoint, the value of knowledge sharing reflects an organizational belief that when workers share knowledge, the organization saves time and resources and prevents reinventing the wheel. The workers also stand to gain by sharing knowledge, and managers should make sure that they realize this fact. The value of knowledge sharing will be embraced by workers when they internalize the benefits it offers, including visibility, attractiveness, recognition, and better chances of promotion. If managers do not believe that knowledge sharing creates benefits for an organization, or if the individuals within the organization do not believe that it is to their benefit to share knowledge, knowledge will not be shared. At BP Amoco, both managers and workers developed an appreciation for the personal and organizational gains associated with sharing knowledge, and those benefits continued to amass over time.

Managers can do a lot to foster the perception of mutual gain from sharing knowledge and promoting it as a behavioral norm.

- First and foremost, they can serve as a personal example. This is probably a major factor at Rafael.
- As was done at BP Amoco, management can make sure to grant time and resources for knowledge sharing to occur. In part, this involves the promotion of *communities of practice*, groups of people who interact in order to share and create knowledge. In Chapter 6, we elaborate on the nature of communities of practice and how they can be managed to promote the value of knowledge sharing.

Another important managerial practice is rewarding knowledge sharing and group effort in addition to providing incentives for solo work. We discuss this point extensively in Chapter 5. In times of economic slowdown, people become increasingly afraid that if they share their knowledge they will make themselves redundant. It is important for managers to realize that under these circumstances, no knowledge management project will succeed. Only if knowledge sharing is rewarded, if the knowledge sharers become heroes or champions, will it become pervasive. When knowledge sharing becomes associated with recognition, individuals have an incentive to share their knowledge.

Another point relates to the moral dimension of culture discussed earlier. Workers are much more likely to share knowledge if they support and identify with the organization's mission and overall values. Identification with the organization's goals fosters a feeling of comfort and safety in sharing one's knowledge with others.

Making Innovation Inherent to Your Organization's Culture

The value of innovation is an inherent part of a knowledge management culture. Innovation as a value is about fostering knowledge creation, rather than merely knowledge sharing. Although Chapter 10 is devoted exclusively to innovation, we would like to also emphasize here that it is a core value underlying managing knowledge to create the organization's future.

Managing current knowledge assets is not a sufficient goal of knowledge management. Organizations need to create new knowledge and innovate in order to create value for the company. Knowledge assets age fast, and overly reusing existing knowledge implies taking the risk that it may become obsolete along the way.

What should a manager do to foster a culture of innovation? The first step is to demand it from yourself and your workers. Feature quarterly reports that include a section looking forward by requiring descriptions of "something new" in the relevant areas of a department's expertise. It may be a new technological achievement, a new process, or new customers. Middle managers usually track the development of these initiatives if they are asked to outline them on a quarterly basis. Beginning with a vague requirement for "something new" may suffice. At later stages you could improve the questions by aligning the "new" with more measurable improvements (more on this in Chapter 10).

Innovation is never a 100 percent sure success. Managers must accept the risks and let knowledge workers (KWs) continue innovating. Some ingredients of a true knowledge culture that a manager should encourage include:

- Situations employing trial and error—sometimes these are the only way to get results quickly.
- Attempts at new methods of doing things and allowing failure, as long as it is the result of positive risk-taking.
- Colleagues to take on local entrepreneurship, and more autonomy so that workers can reach beyond their job descriptions in searching for new knowledge.

Trust and a Win-Win Environment

Trust is both a value that can and should be promoted by the organization's management, and it is the invisible glue that holds together a knowledge managing organizational culture. Without trust, the other values cannot be implemented. Trust is what enables a worker to feel free and safe enough to share his knowledge and to make mistakes on the way to discovery. It also lies behind management's willingness to forego strict control in favor of a more relaxed environment and granting workers free time to interact, ponder, and learn. The value of trust implies that managers and workers believe in the mutual benefits of knowledge management and are willing to embark on the challenge of sharing and creating knowledge together.

This is why a complementary value to trust is the perception of *win-win*. Without a win-win approach, knowledge management won't succeed. Mutual benefits are the key to successful KM, and every knowledge management practice should be implemented with this in mind. Workers should feel that they stand to gain from sharing and creating knowledge.

The following is an example of what can happen when the values of trust and win-win are not internalized. In this case, knowledge management is stifled.

Example: The Kibbutz Member Who Did Not Trust

A kibbutz is a collective community founded on socialist principles. In a kibbutz-owned factory, most of the workers are also members of the community and have deep social bonds outside of work.

In one of Israel's kibbutzim, a chief technologist refused to share his knowledge with the younger chemists who arrived from the university, even though some of these newcomers were the children of his friends. On the surface, it wasn't clear why he should feel threatened by this younger generation, particularly in light of his personal connection to them and membership in the community that owned the factory. But from his perspective, he was afraid to share his knowledge.

He did not trust that the organization would keep him once he shared his knowledge, and he did not see what he stood to gain by sharing it. He thought, "They just want me to teach them what I know and then they will send me home. As long as I have the knowledge, I stay. I'm the troubleshooter. As soon as I start sharing the knowledge, I'm on my way out."

This type of crisis within an organization illustrates two major problems that instilling the right culture of trust and win-win should eliminate:

1. The KW had no trust in the organization. To share knowledge, a KW must feel secure that the organization will continue to value his contribution even after he has trained others.
2. The KW saw knowledge sharing as a win-lose scenario, whereby the organization gains his expertise while he is rendered redundant.

Organizations can turn this perception around, even in times of down-sizing and job insecurity, by illuminating the gains to be had by a knowledge-sharing culture. In this win-win paradigm, when you teach others, you also learn from them. The knowledge, skills, and know-how you gain make you more employable and increase your relative competitive strength in the job market.

We discuss these issues in more detail in Chapter 6.

Tailoring Values to the Company's Knowledge Needs

The values we have discussed so far are fundamental knowledge manage-ment values relevant to every organization: seeking worker knowledge, knowledge sharing, innovation, trust, and so forth. However, success-ful knowledge management in your organization may entail additional values, depending on the particular nature and history of your organization.

Take, for example, the value of speed or agility. Speed is a value for many companies operating in a dynamic market, where time-to-market determines success or failure. It may be less relevant in other companies that value top performance. Essentially, anything that the organization places as foremost is a value. Each organization needs to tailor its culture and values according to its character, industry, and strategic goals.

From Preaching to Practice

Practicing what we preach about values is not very simple or straightfor-ward. How do you define the right culture and values for your organization? How do you assess where you stand relative to them?

Defining the right culture might seem easy, but it is not. Most managers are educated enough to devise some positive-sounding mission statements and declare solid values for the organization. They are also sensitive enough to managerial trends not to outwardly promote a strict and hierar-chical management style.

But let's face it, it's difficult for any manager to self-assess. Many man-agers may not notice the gap that all too often exists between their declared values and how they actually behave. They may not realize they are block-ing their colleagues' contributions. Even if top management does practice what it preaches, middle managers may not (or vice versa). So if we do not know where we are, how will we know where to go? This is where the difficulty lies, and that is what causes the cynical attitude toward values that we've discussed in this chapter.

Awareness and Active Listening

If it is almost impossible to objectively assess our own values and management style, what do we do? Our two best pieces of advice are *awareness* and *active listening*. We hope that reading this chapter has been a major step toward increasing awareness. Active listening has several facets, including these:

■ Ask questions instead of giving directions. Asking questions signals you are appreciating your employees' knowledge and looking for their contribution. Usually you will get the same answers that you would have given, but with the added value of workers' commitment. Sometimes you get better answers. Remember that seeking employees' knowledge is one of the essential values of a KM culture.

■ Applying active listening to the problems in finding core values and creating a better management style does not mean "do it yourself." Make it an organizational discussion of the actual issues and formulate the desired discussion.

■ Ask your employees, colleagues, and superiors about their view on issues. Entrust capable people from your organization to initiate the conversations for you, or hire an organizational consultant, hoping they will be able to pose questions and get frank answers.

■ Have a respectable committee to assimilate the findings into a draft statement of mission and values through consensus.

■ Make sure to get sincere comments on that draft from as many workers as possible (meetings, surveys, etc.)

All in all, this may seem like a long process, but these discussions are necessary to establish the common and shared values accepted by a whole organization.

Conclusion

This chapter on culture concludes the second phase of our KM journey, and completes the groundwork for the knowledge management practices presented in the remainder of this book. If you refer to Figure P.1, you can see that Chapter 2 presented you with the concept of intellectual capital and its value-creating potential; Chapter 3 placed knowledge management within the larger perspective of strategic management; and, finally, this chapter discussed the importance of fostering an organizational culture based on values that promote successful knowledge management.

We feel that the topics from the first few chapters represent the foundation of knowledge management because they provide a broad perspective of the importance of KM and how and why it works. Without this foundation, KM becomes a series of isolated interventions that are doomed to fail. With it, the knowledge management practices presented in the remainder of this book can be implemented for attaining a sustainable competitive advantage.

Now, on to the third phase in the knowledge management journey—description of the various viewpoints of KM, beginning with the central one—the human focus.

The Magnificent 7

1. Becoming a knowledge company entails developing shared values with which workers can identify and a management style that seeks employees' knowledge.
2. The basic building blocks of a knowledge-sharing culture are respect for workers' knowledge, trust, a perception of win-win, and innovation.
3. Many elements of organizational culture that promote knowledge management (including specific values, norms, and management styles) are actually different for each organization in accordance with its character and needs.
4. Managers should conduct a self-assessment to determine the extent to which their culture enhances or stifles knowledge sharing and creation.
5. Managers should identify what is the optimal balance between control and freedom in their organization and actively seek to attain it.
6. It is the manager's responsibility to instill the culture and values that promote and support knowledge management in collaboration with subordinates.
7. Through awareness and active listening, managers can create a culture that seeks each employee's knowledge and contribution.

CHAPTER 5

The Human Focus

Understanding and Managing Knowledge Workers

In this chapter you will:

> Understand that the success of a knowledge company is based on the proper management of its knowledge workers (KWs).
>
> Learn how to make the organization attractive to knowledge workers so that they will be motivated to join and remain.
>
> Gain tools for enlarging the workers' knowledge.
>
> Develop techniques for encouraging knowledge workers to share and contribute their knowledge.

The knowledge worker (KW) is obviously the center, and the main asset, of every organization based on intellectual capital. Managing KWs is one of the core capabilities of an organization. By *managing* we mean all relevant aspects including recruiting and retaining workers, developing their skills and potential, encouraging them to create and share knowledge, and more.

The issue of managing KWs has a very wide scope and appears in many contexts:

- Much of modern thinking on managing human resources (HR) either deals with KWs or promotes similar processes for all workers.

- Almost every aspect of knowledge management requires attention to managing KWs.

We have already discussed the necessary style of management of such workers in the consideration of culture in Chapter 4, and we refer to it in almost every subsequent chapter in this book. In this chapter we focus on issues that involve human resources methods that can be used toward refining the management of knowledge workers.

We begin by discussing the unique identity of the knowledge worker: What is a *knowledge worker*? What are their unique characteristics? Then we describe what happened to KWs during the most recent bubble economies because they served as unique situations in which to examine some of the issues managers invariably come across in managing KWs. Finally, we offer managers practical strategies as well as advice on the implications of issues relating to the effective management of KWs.

Is Every Worker a Knowledge Worker?

When deciding who is a knowledge worker, the usual examples may include researchers and scientists in academia, engineers and software experts in high-tech industries, doctors and nurses in hospitals, smart businessmen and businesswomen who lead revolutions in various branches of the retail market, and others like them. Are all of these, and positions similar to them, the only workers considered to be knowledge workers? There are different views on the subject and after reading this chapter, you can decide what definition is most suitable to characterizing KWs in your organization.

Before we get into the views, we thought we'd mention a couple of Hebrew slang expressions—"big head" versus "small head"—which might inform the discussion, in hopes of arriving at a common definition. In Israel, a "big head" worker is always looking for ways to solve problems creatively within an organization. Rather than just following routines and guidelines to the letter, he takes on more responsibility and decision-making duties than is required by the basic job description. Conversely, a "small head" worker just sticks to his outlined duties consisting of specific tasks, procedures, and a smaller span of authority.

We think every worker in an organization has the capability of being a "big head." Most workers can manage new situations by drawing upon various personal and organizational resources, whether they are at the top or bottom of the ladder. This is becoming more relevant as the world becomes more turbulent and unpredictable.

Any kind of worker can be a "big head," but knowledge workers are required to be so. Managers need to work at "enlarging" the minds of all of their employees to make them into knowledge workers. And, as this chapter illustrates, a managerial style that is too authoritative, strict, and intolerant of initiatives essentially "shrinks" the minds of subordinates, whereas a managerial style that encourages autonomy, trial and error, and creativity "enlarges" the minds of the workers.

The Most Common View: Only Knowledge-Creating and Nonroutine Workers are Knowledge Workers

Many managers believe there is value in making a distinction between knowledge work and manual work. They see a distinction between routine and nonroutine work. Knowledge workers are measured according to how creative they are—how much new knowledge they generate, and how fast they generate it (this is sometimes referred to as *talent management*).

Such managers claim that, although manual workers possess knowledge, ultimately they work on routine tasks. Although they know how to operate the robots in the knowledge-rich industrial organizations for which they work, they are still not the same as knowledge workers who are inventing all the time.

Promoting processes geared to manage knowledge creation and innovation requires a different kind of management style for knowledge workers, as discussed in Chapter 4. This is the group that requires special management attention, as will be discussed later.

Tuvya's View: Almost Every Worker Is a Knowledge Worker

Tuvya opts for a wider definition of knowledge worker. He maintains that if intellectual capital (IC) is the main asset of the organization, then many workers may hold parts of the IC of the company. Here he offers perspective on this question by relaying a story from his work at Rafael, where the issue of defining production workers as manual laborers became an almost explosive one—literally.

Rafael's Explosives Workers

When Rafael was converted from a unit of the government into a government-owned company, many of the company's group contracts had to be revised. Much thought was invested in the new contracts of scientists and researchers and less attention was given to the employees who worked on the (seemingly) simpler manual tasks, like laborers tasked with producing explosive materials.

Initially, top management did not consider the laborers producing the explosives to be valuable knowledge workers. The renewing of contracts seemed like an opportunity to direct many of them into early retirement and/or to replace them with younger, cheaper workers.

(continued)

The middle managers overseeing the laborers of the specific department warned, though, against a possible crisis if the laborers were to
leave. It is true that one doesn't need a university degree for the routine
work they were doing (and working on explosives should definitely
be as prescribed and routine as possible). However, working on explosives does require experience, and their expertise was gained over time.
These longtime laborers at Rafael possessed a unique knowledge, one
that could be seen as crucial for both current ongoing production processes and for researchers developing future processes. After top
managers looked into the knowledge and experience of the laborers,
eventually their contracts were upgraded to reflect their true importance
as being a part of the organizational IC.

The lesson we can learn from Rafael's situation is clear but not trivial.
Although it is true that the core competencies of the organization are
usually held by a relatively small number of knowledge workers, the organization stands to benefit significantly by seeing every worker as a
knowledge worker. Think of customer service clerks with a high-school
education and only a few years of experience in your company. Chances
are that they have knowledge that you want to disseminate into the organization, no matter their background. During their tenure, they have
probably become creative problem solvers, and if they have not, then
you should make sure that they become knowledge creators and knowledge sharers in the future. Knowledge creation and knowledge sharing are
not the exclusive property of R&D departments or only certain types of
workers. You do not want robots working for you. You want creative,
motivated people coming up with initiatives for improving processes no
matter their level.

Knowledge Is in the Eye of the Beholder

A forerunner in IC and KM, Dr. Susan Stucky, manager of the Institute
for Research and Learning (IRL) in Menlo Park, California, adds another
perspective to the debate. She believes that our perception of what a
knowledge organization is, and who its knowledge workers are, may not
coincide with the day-to-day events of a worker's reality. She described
her view in an interview[1] with Tuvya, using the following two examples
from an anthropological study of people at work done at IRL by Dr. Brigitte
Jordan.[2]

Both of Brigitte Jordan's studies examined routine work processes
(i.e., without much invention or creativity occurring). But in spite of this,

The Dynamics of Medical Teams during Births

The first example reviewed an obstetrics ward and how not all knowledge collected was used or shared. The mother-to-be was the central figure in this example. Nurses usually spent many hours with the women and gained important knowledge about them and their individual cases. However, in the end, the nurses ended up having less decision-making power than the doctors who were treating the patients when it came to the birth. Often the knowledge they accumulated during their time together was not considered to be as relevant as the doctor's when it came to the actual birth, and many times their knowledge did not even reach the doctors. In this example, the doctors were the final authority and decision makers, even though they did not necessarily have all of the pertinent knowledge.

The Dynamics of Teams Working on Passenger Jets

The second study examined various kinds of teams working in an airport, preparing a passenger jet for take-off. These teams worked together, helping each other reach solutions to common problems having to do with maintenance, logistics, food, luggage, and much more. A lot of information flowed directly between workers—without the mediation or involvement of the manager—using open radio channels or in group discussion. While there was a formal hierarchy, most decisions were made collaboratively based on relevant data available to all.

Stucky and Jordan point out how the airline teams actually engaged in more knowledge management processes than did the hospital workers. This goes against what one would normally assume considering doctors and nurses, because they are generally thought of as important knowledge workers in a strong, KM-minded organization. Nevertheless, the airline made better use of its human capital by valuing the cumulative knowledge of its workers.

Obviously this debate was not included to confuse the reader but to illustrate the various kinds and levels of knowledge workers in various organizations. Managers need to customize their definitions of KWs, and the methods of improving their overall knowledge-creation and knowledge-sharing processes, in order to tailor them to the specific needs of the organization and the people within it.

Shaking Up the Balance of Power: Lessons from the First Bubble Crisis

The issues of managing knowledge workers are well illustrated by the two most recent bubble economies. From the point of view of KWs, we see that both bubbles were characterized by start-ups luring KWs from established companies by offering them inflated salaries and even more inflated job descriptions. The following two examples demonstrate the most important lessons learned. (By the way, such economic crises are bad for employers and employees but good for book authors! Seriously, though, they do magnify certain types of problems and make solutions clearer than in more stable times.)

Here, Tuvya recalls some anecdotes from the first bubble crisis in Israel, many of which are probably typical for knowledge companies globally, especially when going through chaotic KW transitions.

Lesson 1: The Breach of Trust

Tuvya's first anecdote demonstrates the inflated salary offers at that time and their influence on the mutual trust between employers and employees:

The Temptation of Inflated Salaries

In the early 2000s, my son, then a fresh university graduate, got a job in a high-tech start-up. Surprisingly, his salary and benefits were quite similar to my own, despite the fact that I was holding a senior position at Rafael after several decades of experience in the industry.

As in many other companies at the time, some departments in Rafael were severely affected by start-ups leaching talent away with these exaggerated offers. Departments with knowledge workers in high-tech professions (software engineers, electronic communications experts, and algorithm developers), that were courted extensively by start-ups and were hit badly at the time.

Because Rafael was then a government unit, it could not be as competitive with salaries as the start-up groups. Trying to convince people to stay by mentioning the advantages of Rafael in both technology and tenure was ineffective with young engineers, who were being offered twice the salary and a better title than what they could get at Rafael with years of experience. Even older engineers were ready to forgo the benefits of their tenured jobs rather than pass up what they saw as the opportunity of a lifetime.

The breach of mutual trust may be a possible insight from the experience of the first bubble. Knowledge workers become increasingly mobile, moving from organization to organization, from project to project, based on where the higher salary and/or professional interest lie. Loyalty to the organization seems a thing of the past. In those years, small start-ups lured workers with stock options and dreams of instant wealth. Some of the larger organizations found themselves with an acute shortage of workers in the middle of a project, with deadlines looming. The workers' lack of identification with the organization's goals was a clear breach of trust.

In light of the ensuing slowdown in the high-tech industries, however, it appears as if the tables had turned. With numerous start-ups going under, the larger, more stable organizations were in a powerful position vis-à-vis the worker. And unfortunately, some were abusing this power and acting in trust-violating ways. For example, some U.S. aerospace industries have undergone massive layoffs, often letting go of employees who spent many years specializing in professional areas that are specifically suited to the company. The layoffs were claimed to be inevitable, but other companies, such as Southwest Airlines, opted to cut costs in other ways, including salary cuts, rather than breach the mutual trust they had worked so hard to establish.

This sad insight, while not giving immediate clues as to how to manage KWs, is nevertheless important as a perpetual warning for both sides:

- Employees now understand better the advantages of working in stable organizations as opposed to volatile start-ups.
- Organizations have learned to keep investing in their employees in both good times and bad.

LESSON 2: THE IMPORTANCE AND MOBILITY OF KNOWLEDGE WORKERS Tuvya's second anecdote demonstrates the special importance of knowledge workers:

The Fight on KW: Intel versus Rafael versus Start-Ups

During the crisis, there was tension between Rafael and the Israeli branch of Intel Corporation. While not competing in terms of customers, Rafael and Intel Israel competed when it came to knowledge workers. A team leader from Rafael ended up leaving for a job at Intel and later convinced about 10 other electronic engineers from his team to join him at the new branch, thus almost completely closing an important knowledge center at Rafael. Eventually, reconciliatory talks between Intel and Rafael led the then manager of Intel Israel, Mooly

(continued)

Eden, to visit Rafael and give an unforgettable lecture on the hemor-
rhaging of employees to competitive start-ups.

In the speech it turned out that, while Rafael was suffering in only
a few departments, Intel was in a much worse situation overall. Being
in the core of the high-tech industry, almost all Intel workers were prone
to courtship by an array of start-ups. Many Intel workers were strongly
tempted, and the ramifications of their workers leaving were much more
widespread at Intel than at Rafael.

While start-ups were portrayed as the bad guys, their quest for KWs
was not easy, either. Imagine a well-intentioned entrepreneur, finally
receiving money from an investor to develop his brilliant idea but
having no engineer to work with. And imagine the extra frustration,
after finding such an engineer, to see him leaving after several months
for a better-paying employer.

The lesson here is unforgettable: Knowledge workers are the main
assets of the organization and are not easily replaced. Sometimes just one
of them abandoning the organization may cause a disaster, let alone more
than one of them leaving.

Knowledge workers have a high mobility as their expertise is usually
desired by other organizations and especially by competitors. Hence they
have lots of opportunities outside your organization and should be cherished. You cannot force KWs to stay, but you must make them want to
stay. This is a difficult mission for managers.

The Aftermath

The aftermath of the high-tech bubble was ugly. Many start-ups collapsed,
especially those that didn't have a firm business strategy. Upon collapsing,
obviously their KWs were laid off (including Tuvya's son). Major existing
companies also had difficult times. Some of them, like Southwest Airlines
and Applied Materials, tried to save their KWs by reducing salaries and
taking other cost-cutting measures. Others, like some aerospace companies,
seized the opportunity to lay off workers. Because times are so chaotic
during economic bubbles, we cannot entirely rely on them to examine
conventional HR practices, but we can use the circumstances to study how
relations change between KWs and their employers when times are tough.

Lessons learned from the first bubble include the culmination of a
change in the psychological contract between KWs and their employers.
The psychological contract represents all of their beliefs about the nature
of their employment relationship. In the prebubble days, the psychological

contract outlined that employers were caretakers of the employees. Employees who were good performers were guaranteed a job until their retirement and were offered career paths within the organization. In return, employees were loyal and committed to the job and the organization over the long term.

Post-bubble, the new psychological contract outlines that organizations no longer have to offer long-term employment. Employees are responsible for their own career development. Their commitment to the work and their professional development has been replaced with a short-term commitment to the job and to the organization for however long they are there. The new contract implies that when workers contribute their knowledge, they expect to gain something in return, especially increased employability.

The concepts of employability and the need to retain KWs are both crucial for the success of an organization. Exploring these concepts leads to important advice about managing KWs. We elaborate on this at the end of this chapter.

Lessons from the Second Bubble Crisis

The second bubble, while having colossal impacts on the world economy, was more benign from the point of view of the high-tech industry in Israel. It was significant enough to require specific action regarding retention of knowledge workers, yet small enough to examine the effectiveness of the conventional HR methods we would use in regular times.

Lesson 1: Retain Your Leading KWs

The upside of the second bubble began in Israel at the end of 2007 and the beginning of 2008. It was more pronounced in real estate and financial institutions, just like in the rest of the world, but some prosperity also began to show in the high-tech sector.

Tuvya recalls the threats of that temporary prosperity on retaining knowledge workers, and how they were tackled:

Rafael Efforts to Retain Leading KW

In the upside of the second bubble, early 2007, it took some time to identify that there was a problem. At Rafael, probably like in any other large organization, there is always talk about the grass being greener

(continued)

(and salaries being higher) on the other side. But eventually it was clear that the number of workers approached by outside employers, offering generous salaries, was larger than usual, and we asked ourselves, "what should we do?"

The initial remedy against the second bubble's effects was learning from the lessons of the first. Workers of all ages still remembered the gloomy times of the high-tech bubble and were more reluctant to leave a stable organization and an interesting job for a dubious future, even when offered higher salaries and/or fancy titles.

But learning from history was not enough, and we took some additional proactive action. When a worker begins to shop outside for a job it may be too late. So we identified our leading knowledge workers (the "talent," especially those in professions desirable to outside companies), and worked in two ways to ensure they were happy with us:

- *Compensation.* We examined salaries and upgraded those who were lower when compared to the relevant market. A small raise, initiated by the employer, has a greater positive effect than a higher raise requested by the worker to match an outside offer.
- *Job satisfaction.* Middle managers were required to talk with leading KWs and make sure they were happy with their jobs. Do they like their current project assignments or are they bored with them? Do they wish to continue doing professional work or want a management position or other career path? The findings required us to make some changes.

The result: Almost no people left during the second bubble, at least not above the usual rate (which is usually very low in Rafael).

The actions taken are actually almost the same used as part of a healthy, regular routine in HR's management of every worker. The bubble simply required us to perform them more frequently for the selected leading KWs.

Lesson 2: Recruit More Leading KWs

Rafael also tried to exploit the downsizing occurring in other companies as a result of the second bubble by using it as an opportunity to recruit some high-profile KWs, with some surprising results.

As many readers know, the world economic crisis began in autumn of 2008 and has continued into 2010. We are not going to speculate how and when it might finally end, but Israel's economy has survived quite well. Nevertheless, there were some layoffs and caution among new investments.

But as Rafael had a rather successful year in 2009, the managers were thinking the second bubble was an opportunity for recruiting stars who were leaving less successful companies. The following is Tuvya's experience:

Are the Stars Out There?

We were naively thinking there were many star KWs out there, laid off from various failing companies. Unfortunately our search did not yield lots of success. Yes, for every open position, junior or senior, there were more applicants than usual. But "stars," and even only "very good" KWs, were quite rare.

We suspect that most companies that did not collapse were doing their best to retain their stars, and the "very good" KWs were sticking to their job, hesitating to make a bold move.

Hence, from the point of view as a manager in Rafael, Tuvya was disappointed at the lack of recruits he could gain from the shakeup. But from a KM point of view he was happy to realize many companies had learned a lesson from the first bubble: Although they are in trouble, they are trying to hold on to their leading KWs.

The Aftermath

Regarding the management of KWs, the lessons learned from the second bubble crisis are less dramatic than the first. However, they are more optimistic and more relevant to a KW's day-to-day behavior. Lessons from the first bubble were reemphasized in the second, and both KWs and employers learned something valuable:

- KWs should be more cautious about leaving a stable job.
- Employers should be more cautious about laying off KWs even in difficult times.

Overall, these lessons should be used as methods of managing KWs in regular times as well as economically challenging ones.

The Challenge of Retention

The previous examples establish the challenge of attracting and retaining knowledge workers. Organizations spend considerable resources in an effort to hold on to workers with important knowledge, and yet the high turnover rate among these workers remains. Organizations compete for quality workers just as they compete for customers, and they need to invest the same kind of creative effort with their workforce as they do in marketing and sales promotion. In light of constraints on an organization's ability to raise salaries, we need to apply other concepts as well.

Just like customers, workers differ greatly from each other in their needs. Organizations can apply the concept of customization from the world of the customers to the world of human resources. Whereas some workers are concerned about salary, others want more free time, others desire to study, and still others need to meet family obligations. The organization will benefit from exhibiting flexibility in meeting its workers' needs.

Usually knowledge workers have personal contracts, where both employer and employee can untie their relationship at will. Actually there are some checks and balances that usually stabilize these relations and enable knowledge culture. But we have seen that in some situations, like the bubble crises, these checks and balances fail.

Retention Tactics

Organizations can experiment with different kinds of links to KWs, some of which are loose and others which are more binding. We will mention two of them here while summarizing that the challenge of retention always exists, no matter what the form of contract between the employer and the KW.

- *Tenure.* The old system of tenure for lifetime employment still exists in some places: academia, government institutions, and also businesses in some countries. Rafael, for instance, employs it. Tenure can be both great and devastating for knowledge management. On the one hand, it enables the trust required for a positive knowledge culture. But, on the other, it may allow employees to languish, which limits management's flexibility in pushing an employee to do his best.

- *Options.* The modern, well-known practice of offering a worker stock options renders the worker a partner, while simultaneously confining him to only benefiting when the company benefits. The worker many times remains in the organization not because he enjoys the work but because he does not want to miss the opportunity to exercise the options.

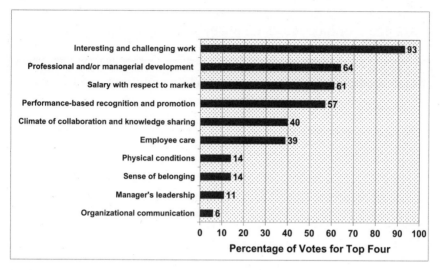

FIGURE 5.1 Relative Importance of Various Elements of Job Satisfaction
Source: Rafael Advanced Defense Systems Ltd.

Is Salary a Main Factor?

If you conduct an informal survey, the majority of responders will probably answer yes. Unfortunately, we have seen many veteran managers think the same.

But knowledge workers think otherwise! Anonymous surveys checking on job satisfaction at Rafael were conducted among thousands of workers. Figure 5.1 shows the typical results in one department when employees were asked, "What are the top four factors affecting your job satisfaction?" Employees stated "interesting job" as the main factor keeping them at their jobs—93 percent of responders put it in the top four! Further, from the results, we can see that salary was not even one of the leading two factors—and 40 percent did not put it in their top four! Other knowledge organizations worldwide usually report similar responses: Salary is not the main factor affecting job satisfaction. This should lead managers to consider taking care of the other important indicators like encouraging work on interesting assignments, and so on.

However, managers should beware of using such surveys as an excuse not to care enough about the salary of knowledge workers. In 1997, a report from the Israeli State Comptroller demonstrated what happened when managers put too little emphasis on salary:[3]

Obviously, KWs consider appropriate salary, in a scale comparable to the relevant market, as a necessary condition to their job satisfaction. Only

Example: An Electronics Company with an Outdated Salary Scale

A government-owned company,* specializing in aerospace electronics, had a promising book value as indicated by decent profits and a reasonable backlog of orders. The State Comptroller noticed, however, numerous anomalies in the structure of the workforce: An inadequate salary scale resulted in aging engineers within the company receiving higher salaries than engineers hired through a manpower firm, whereas young engineers were paid less than their external peers.

Not surprisingly, this illogical system resulted in a self-sustained destructive process, whereby young engineers were not attracted to the company. The aging R&D force was gradually losing touch with the latest advances in technological innovation.

---

*Not Rafael.

when this condition is fulfilled will they look at job satisfaction as the discriminating factor. In the following section, we present some factors affecting job satisfaction.

Keeping KWs Interested Throughout Their Career

We have already shown that knowledge workers must have interesting and challenging work in order to be effective and productive. They need an intellectual challenge, otherwise they suffer. We assume an organization fulfills this prerequisite at the start, and then we try to help it avoid the pitfalls that may change an otherwise great workplace into a boring routine.

What makes one's work interesting is not fixed and permanent. It can vary among different KWs, and it may change for the same person in different stages of his career. Inadequate assignment, or neglecting career development, may make a good KW unmotivated and/or drive him to leave. The goal of this section is to share experiences about such pitfalls and show your organization how to avoid them.

Edna confirms that small organizations cater to changes in a KW's preferences and hopes for a career path. She says:

> *We sometimes recruit university graduates who serve as assistants to our senior consultants while learning their job's skills. After a few years of experience, and usually another degree, these consultants then have*

their own assistants who relieve them from routine work. The young and inexperienced workers are happy to be assistants and learn from the more senior consultants, and the latter enjoy the ability to focus on the more interesting part of their tasks.

For a small firm, continuous growth is a must or people will outgrow their job and leave for positions outside the firm. When a larger organization faces similar problems, it might use different solutions due to the differing environment and scale. Larger organizations have both larger obligations and larger opportunities for career development. They usually like to retain KWs for many years, and have a variety of opportunities to offer them. A KW usually begins as a young university graduate, learning the basics of his profession in school and then continuing along one of two basic paths:

1. The professional path. A KW may continue developing his expertise as a professional. An organization will usually invest in advanced training, encouraging him to study for a master's degree or PhD, and involve him with ever-increasing and renewed challenges. Many organizations award their experts appropriate titles, like "professional fellow," in recognition of their importance to the knowledge organization.

2. The management path. The KW may move to any of the many managing positions a large organization has available, managing groups of professionals ranging from small teams to larger departments, leading projects, moving from R&D to manufacturing and vice versa.

These paths are not totally separate. Some KWs will likely move from one path to the other and back along their career. In a knowledge organization, for instance, most managing positions usually require some professional experience.

MAKE EVERY ASSIGNMENT INTERESTING OR MEANINGFUL   It is a challenge to assure every KW's assignments are interesting. Again, we assume most of the work an employee does is attractive to him. But what do we do with the less attractive parts?

Edna offers a rather simple solution she's found from managing her consulting firm. She says that she offers consultants the opportunity to work on projects that interest them. If a project is not assigned, it is outsourced. Thus consultants do not find themselves working on tasks that they don't want to do.

In a large organization you cannot always use Edna's method of looking for volunteers for every assignment and outsourcing what is rejected. Tasks are usually interdisciplinary and people collaborate with many others. Everyone wants new, exciting projects, but there are always less attractive, more routine projects that are equally important.

Fortunately, in a properly managed knowledge organization, there are many complementary methods to cope with this problem.

- *Achieve commitment.* When workers are committed to an organization, and to its current project, they will be ready to do the more boring and routine parts of the work. Workers should feel that they serve a mission and that they contribute to a whole, though their goals should be reevaluated along the life of their career path.
- *Incorporate the full life cycle of a project as a necessary professional experience.* In order to grow up as an expert knowledge worker, you need to go through all the various phases of a project. At Rafael, projects go on for years, and KWs participate in them from preliminary studies through detailed design to final tests. Thus a KW experiences the full circle of design and the lessons learned, undertaking both fascinating and tedious parts alike.
- *Change a KW's job.* Moving from one position to another every several years stops the feeling of routine and injects new motivation and new challenges into a KW's daily work. When a KW is advancing from team member to team leader, even though he may be doing the same kind of work, he is getting new perspectives and new interests. This emphasizes the importance of establishing career paths, as discussed earlier.
- *Enrich a routine or make it a reserve duty.* Engineers usually prefer to develop new products rather than provide technical support for the departments manufacturing or maintaining old ones. However, these departments, which usually create most of the sales and profits for the company, must have expert technical support. At Rafael, they have responded to this type of situation using two methods:
  1. Keep the engineering personnel in manufacturing departments to a minimum, consisting mainly of people whose expertise and interest are in general manufacturing processes.
  2. Solve technical problems in manufacturing specific products by temporary mobilizations of the best engineers who had developed that old product, even though they are now working on a new product. Mobilizing the best engineers assures the best solution for manufacturing the old product, while keeping such duties in reserve for a short time is not devastating to the new product and does not hamper worker motivation.

In conclusion, we see that there are many methods to help enrich assignments that are unpopular with KWs. It's much like the saying about changing diapers: No one enjoys it, but when it is your baby, it somehow becomes a part of the joy of parenthood.

CREATE AND MAINTAIN A FULL KNOWLEDGE MATRIX   One of the main goals of managing KWs is to avoid a situation where an entire organization is relying on one person, or a small clique of experts, who solely hold the critical knowledge of the organization.

In Chapter 1, we described the case of Nathan, the irreplaceable technician. He was the only one who knew how to maintain an old simulator that was essential to his department's work. When he decided to retire, his managers faced a knowledge vacuum in a critical organizational function.

Edna has run across similar phenomena in some of her client's organizations, and has identified it not only as extremely dangerous for an organization, but also as very bad for KWs themselves. While some enjoy this source of power, others understand that being stuck in the same activity hampers their professional development. Hence it contradicts the "keep them interested" mantra mentioned previously.

The situation of irreplaceable employees may be prevented if management continually checks the knowledge matrix of the organization or its various departments. The rows of this matrix consist of a list of the various competencies of the department, and the columns are the names of the employees. Whenever you have only one employee holding the knowledge of some competence, you are in trouble. In many cases you might even want more than two.

Although keeping the knowledge matrix full seems obvious, one usually finds all kinds of understandable but unjustified objections:

- For the manager, and their clients, it is always more convenient to keep the knowledge of certain products or processes all under the same veteran.
- Similarly, a KW with a power position may be reluctant to share his knowledge, and other KWs may not want to learn old stuff.

However, all parties—managers, clients, and KWs—must understand that investing in an effort to increase the knowledge matrix now will eventually yield an enormous force multiplier for all of them. It is a must for long-term survival of an organization. If you do it early enough you will encounter less resistance for knowledge sharing down the road, and you may even find your KWs have more enthusiasm for learning new things.

Show Interest in Your Knowledge Workers

Top management must show interest in their knowledge workers (their *talent*), even if they are not direct subordinates. This message is usually true for any kind of worker, but it is especially important for KWs. This acquaintance satisfies a KW's need for recognition and makes them more secure about their future role in the organization.

REGULAR MEETINGS WITH KNOWLEDGE WORKERS   Having regular meetings with KWs is one way to strengthen the bond between managers and KWs. Such meetings may be formal or informal, as described in the following examples:

Cellcom's CEO Informal Meetings

Amos Shapira, CEO of Cellcom, the largest cellular phone company in Israel, tells about his informal way of keeping acquainted with Cellcom's leading KWs:[4]

> *"I cannot imagine a situation in which I am the only one who suggests ideas. Workers, even the most junior ones, have lots of knowledge and experience and should get every chance to express them. This is why I always hang around in the corridors and near coffee machines, and during lunch I sit with the workers and not with the managers (who do not like to eat with me [their boss] anyway . . .). However, it is not enough for a CEO to be available and hang around the workers. If you do not look friendly enough—who will approach you?"*

Rafael Manager's Formal Weekly Visits

The late Gadi Barak managed a division of about 1,000 workers at Rafael. He used to conduct a weekly visit to one of the sections in his division (about 40 people). He brought along to these two-hour visits an entire management team.

The goal of the visit was to maintain a two-way communication, and a major part of the visit consisted of engineers and scientists presenting their current work. The exposure created rapport among the managers and its leading KWs.

SPECIAL CARE OF STAR WORKERS   Some companies take special care of their star KWs, including giving them exposure to corporate management. However, it must be carried out carefully in order not hamper the delicate balance between top management, middle management, and the star KWs themselves. The following are some examples to illustrate the issue:

Pinpointing the Stars

A global semiconductor corporation headquartered in Europe, with about 45,000 employees worldwide, decided in 2003 to define its top employees as a special elite group. This group of about 500 people consisted mostly of star knowledge workers and some potential executives.

The stars in this group were removed from the responsibility of the local managers in their country, and were managed by a special unit in the central headquarters location, reporting to the CEO. The rationale was that local managers might hamper the advancement of these stars because of various local interests, while a central unit with global perspective would do a better job in taking care of them.

Initially the group idea was a success. The stars were receiving training, personal development, mentoring, and special benefits. They were invited to conferences with top management and enjoyed the personal attention, elevating their performance and motivation.

Eventually, however, the experiment failed. The central unit could not really take care of the people in local situations, and it was in continuous conflict with local management. Most members of this international group of stars were eventually confused by being managed both locally and centrally, and the experiment was discontinued.

Interviewing the Stars

In early 2000, Rafael's CEO asked his managers to identify the 50 brightest and most promising scientists. He recognized that the organization's future depended on the brilliant workers and accordingly began taking personal care of them. He interviewed each one of them about their feelings, their expectations and how they were being met, and their desires and needs.

There was a debate about the effectiveness of this action. The attention made the KWs feel special and probably contributed to preventing some of them from being tempted to leave the company during the first bubble. However, division managers and other middle managers resented being circumvented, and claimed it confused KWs.

Overall, star KWs are a key asset of an organization, and both top managers and middle managers must ensure their development and satisfaction. Exposure of KWs to the CEO and top management is an important part of managing them. However, even the brightest KWs must have only one manager at a given time. Ultimately it is the middle managers who should be following the progress of these workers, while the CEO and top management should make sure the middle managers are managing their teams effectively.

Keeping in Touch with Knowledge Workers Who Leave

When the employment relationship ends, organizations stand to benefit from maintaining contact with their former workers.

Retiring Knowledge Workers

A simple case is with people who have reached retirement age after a long-term service with a company. Most successful KM companies keep in touch with retiring workers, especially when they are the top KWs. Here are two examples from Monsanto and Rafael.

In a 1997 interview, Bipin Junnarkar (formerly head of knowledge management architecture at Monsanto) relayed that Monsanto requested a select number of its retiring experts to continue their relationship with the company:

> *They did not have a full-time job, but were expected to work one or two days a week on average as consultants. They were given laptop computers and access to the company's intranet and e-mail so they could work off-site. Whenever there was a problem and their advice was needed, they were contacted by the company. They were paid for their work, but the retirees also said their main compensation was of feeling rewarded from the intellectual interest and staying challenged after retirement.*[5]

Similarly, Rafael employed a system like Monsanto's (but without some of the technological perks like laptops). Initially, many Rafael retirees volunteered to continue working in a consulting capacity with the company. This went on for years but eventually evolved into a Monsanto-style system: Those who were really needed, and worked particularly hard, got paid through a partial employment arrangement.

Alumni Networks

A seemingly more complicated case is when a worker leaves in the middle of his career, for a different job or even to a competitor. However, it still would benefit an organization to develop an alumni network—actual or virtual—with him (just like universities do with their graduating students). Such an alumni network would be available to help the organization with questions or concerns regarding knowledge or finding the right contacts whenever needed.

Edna offers this example from running her consulting business:

Being the owner of a small organization, I must accept that some workers will eventually leave. However, I was a little disappointed when a capable and likeable worker told me that he did not want to continue being a consultant. Although he could continue with us, he wanted to become a marketing manager and began looking for a job.

Instead of stalling his benefits and advancement, I chose to help him. I redefined his role as marketing manager for my office, to help him receive experience in the relevant field. He eventually left, but remained a friend that I will always be able to count on later.

Rewarding Knowledge Creation and Sharing

Is knowledge creation and dissemination something that managers should reward? Or should the organization see it as a basic obligation of the employee that does not require additional incentives? We present two extreme answers to this question.

On one end, Patricia Seemann, formerly director of knowledge management at Hoffmann-La Roche, thinks that knowledge belongs to the organization.[6] Hence sharing is a basic obligation of the employee. If a knowledge worker does not share his knowledge, he is essentially stealing from the company.

At the other end of the spectrum are some union leaders. They claim that workers are human capital and they own the knowledge. Thus if management wants to make changes or lay off employees, they believe they should pay the workers for the knowledge they have accumulated.

We are not going to elaborate on this debate because the answer is probably somewhere in the middle. There must be some form of reward but it is up to the employer and the KW to settle on the terms, whether psychological or in the form of monetary compensation. Rewarding cannot be decoupled from related subjects discussed in other chapters of this book, however, such as:

- Maintaining a positive culture plays a major part in motivating knowledge creation and sharing (Chapter 4).
- The means toward creating healthy space for interactions of knowledge creation and sharing usually have some element of reward and recognition (Chapter 6).

With that said, here are some examples of how to reward such behavior.

Example: The Academia Way

In academia, there is a very decisive method of reward for creating and sharing knowledge: "Publish or perish." At universities, there is a direct relationship between how much knowledge you create or share and your possibility of promotion. Eligibility for promotion is usually decided upon by a committee of peers, including recommendations from experts outside the university.

Can we use such a system in the industrial or business environment? There are not too many existing examples to learn from, though Rafael did employ such a program at one time. In a semi-academic promotion system for KWs, it required the work done by an employee to be documented in technical reports. The KWs' promotions were then based on the quality of their work, as evidenced by the reports and assessed by experts both inside and outside the company.

The system definitely rewarded and encouraged knowledge creation, sharing, and codification, as described later in Chapter 7. However, it had some major disadvantages: It moved some of the authority for promotion from the company manager to external experts, and ultimately underestimated the importance of teamwork and/or management assignment (because employees were being evaluated independent of those things).

The system was eventually abandoned when Rafael transformed from a government unit into a government-owned company with different work contracts. While we see the positives of the heritage of some past practices at Rafael—like some of the major contributors to its knowledge culture—we cannot recommend such semi-academic reward systems in a business environment.

Types of Compensation

When you do choose a reward system, you can choose among a few different types in order to encourage knowledge creation and sharing. Some examples include hard (or explicit) compensation and soft compensation.

Hard compensation can entail incentives such as:

- *Bonuses*. IBM offers a bonus package that is shared between those who create knowledge and those who use it. Skandia used to give bonuses according to the extent a department met its IC indicators, and the system included some valuation of the knowledge creation aspects of KWs' jobs in addition to their financial performance.
- *Access to others' knowledge and data*. At Toyota, knowledge about production is available to all of the component suppliers in return for their knowledge and data.
- *Promotion*. In many large consulting companies, a consultant is promoted to partner based on peer recommendations regarding the extent of his knowledge-creation and knowledge-sharing capabilities.

Soft compensation can entail incentives such as:

- *Community membership*. Some organizations offer employees the opportunity to be a part of knowledge communities, in which knowledge is shared with everyone within their group.
- *Establishing a personal reputation among peers*. This can be an important soft motivator. Studies have found that placing emphasis on researchers' publications in pharmaceutical development companies raises the number of new products that are introduced in the market.
- *Personal gratification from helping others*. Some people really enjoy teaching and helping others and use this as their motivation, nurtured by their employers, in helping to create an environment rich in knowledge sharing.

Conclusion

This chapter dealt with the most important concept in knowledge management—the knowledge worker. We learned that ideally we can strive to make any kind of worker a knowledge worker (a "big head"), but we will usually have a more unique group of workers constituting the human capital of an organization.

We then described the challenges of retaining these types of workers in good times and bad. Retaining KWs requires the continuous attention of managers at all levels of an organization. Managers must continuously ensure that KWs are kept busy with interesting and challenging work, that they receive recognition and credit for it, and that their compensation is appropriate. We hope you can use the examples we've given here to respond to challenges you might face and customize them to the environment of your own organization.

The next chapters deal with additional concepts important to KM, all connected to the human focus.

The Magnificent 7

1. Although any kind of worker can be a knowledge worker, knowledge workers have unique characteristics that stem from their need to be creative and the nonroutine nature of their work.
2. Organizations compete for quality workers just as they compete for customers, and they need to invest the same kind of creative effort as they do in marketing and sales promotion in attracting knowledge workers.
3. The two bubble economies, of early 2000s and late 2000s, demonstrate the challenges of retaining KWs.
4. The organization must keep its KWs interested and challenged throughout their career.
5. When workers share their knowledge, they expect some kind of compensation in return. Managers can provide both hard and soft types of compensation.
6. Managers should prevent situations in which one person alone holds critical knowledge. They also need to make sure when they downsize that they keep those workers who hold key knowledge.
7. When the employment relationship ends, organizations should maintain contact with their workers and continue to tap their knowledge through alumni networks and hiring them as freelancers and consultants.

CHAPTER 6

Managing Interactions for Knowledge Creation and Sharing

In this chapter you will:

> Learn that knowledge creation and sharing occurs primarily through social interactions within communities.
>
> Understand the manager's role in promoting interactions and removing personal and organizational barriers that hinder interactions as the basic means of knowledge management.
>
> Gain specific tools for building the infrastructure and implementing the processes to promote these interactions.

Interactions via formal and casual meetings or via other numerous forms are the primary arena for knowledge creation and sharing. This is because by interacting with one another, people not only *share* ideas but also generate new ones that they would not have come up with if they were engaged in the tasks alone. Thus, we claim that managers should expend considerable effort toward facilitating these interactions: encouraging, promoting, and nurturing them.

The necessity of interactions is not obvious to everyone, as the following typical debate at Rafael shows:

CoP Meetings—a Must or a Waste of Time?

Michael, a department manager who is responsible for several sections, has been complaining that one of his section leaders "insists on wasting two hours a week on unnecessary section meetings." At these meetings, Michael complains, "All twenty busy section members spend precious time talking about who knows what, with no immediate benefit, while doing nothing to meet their own tight deadlines."

"But," Michael's colleague Saul reminds him, "this is the very same section leader you recently recommended for an award! I recall you boasting that he has built an outstanding section. You may also recall that in another section, which you consider the worst in your department, the leader never holds section meetings. Is it so unreasonable to imagine that the opportunity for people to get together and talk is beneficial and maybe even obligatory for the success of the section?"

You probably guess that we side with Saul on this debate. This chapter is dedicated to convincing you of the importance of interactions and shows numerous methods to encourage them.

We begin with an explanation of the social context of knowledge creation and sharing and explain why these must happen through interactions. We also discuss the barriers that may prevent them, such as the conflicting demands on employees' time. Essentially, we claim that managing knowledge is about managing interactions within communities of knowledge workers.

The manager plays a key role in promoting and enhancing these interactions. He must support both one-on-one interactions and group activities within knowledge communities. Hence the chapter continues to describe and discuss various methods and techniques that managers can utilize to achieve these ends. We offer numerous examples of organizations that increased the extent of knowledge creation and sharing by managing interaction communities.

The Social Model for Knowledge Creation and Sharing

In various organizations around the world, skilled and highly regarded managers unknowingly use an assortment of methods to manage the social aspects of knowledge processes, without a systematic understanding of the secret of their success. Fostering knowledge sharing and creating through interactions between workers is essential to any practical implementation of knowledge management. But successful implementation hinges on an understanding of why these methods work or fail.

Tacit Knowledge

The reason that interactions are so important for knowledge management is that they allow for the exchange and creation of tacit knowledge. *Tacit* knowledge is different from *explicit* knowledge, which is documented or written in a codified and explicit form. Tacit knowledge is inside people's heads. Tacit knowledge is expressed in responding to new situations and problems, thus creating new knowledge (which you may later codify).

The most effective way to acquire tacit knowledge is in learning by doing. Often tacit knowledge is disseminated in dyadic (one-on-one) situations, in which newcomers to a job learn the ropes of their new role. Mentoring programs often formalize the process (we expand on mentoring in Chapter 7). Another way is to enable everybody, who may not be new in the organization but new to a specific problem, to tap the experience and tacit knowledge of the best experts in the organization (see the later section on "Yellow Pages").

Communities of Practice—the Basic Instrument of Knowledge Creation and Sharing

Communities of practice (CoPs) are a social model whose basic claim is that learning, innovation, and collaboration are social processes. Hence the creation of new tacit knowledge is usually achieved through interactions in forums larger than the dyad, and is best performed in CoPs.

CoPs are networks of people who have common interests, share a field of specialization, have known each other over a period of time, and trust each other. Therefore it is natural and easy for them to share and create new knowledge, either as a group or as individuals inspired by the group.

The CoPs may have different forms:

- They may be formal, like a successful professional team of mechanical engineers in an organization, or informal, like a group of middle managers from various departments of the organization with some common interests.
- A person may belong to several CoPs, like the mechanical engineer from the previous example who is also a middle manager.
- They can usually be identified. However, they may be difficult to manage, especially if they are not a formal team.

Making the most out of CoPs requires managers to enact sophisticated tactics that reflect an understanding of the social processes of knowledge creation and sharing, and how these processes operate in their organizations. An example of one of the oldest organizations making good use of the CoPs concept is Oxford University (although its founders probably never heard the term *CoPs*) shows:

Oxford University's Communities of Practice

Oxford is a brand name in the academic world, for a reason. For 800 years, Oxford University has been managing its knowledge in an exemplary manner. What is the secret of its success? Part of the answer lies in enabling knowledge interactions.

Oxford students are simultaneous members of two knowledge communities, both of which are intensely nurtured by the university. On one hand they are members of an academic department, such as political science, literature, chemistry, or economics. These departments host seminars and tutorials for transmitting knowledge in a discipline and researching new areas. On the other hand, every student and faculty member belongs to a college, which is a close-knit interdisciplinary community. In the colleges, members study, teach, eat, and live together. They participate in special activities in the evenings and on weekends. Historians share ideas with medical students; law students discuss legal issues with mathematicians. Within each of these knowledge communities, students and faculty engage in frequent interactions of knowledge sharing and creating.

These interactions raise the chances for each person to break free from narrow disciplinary conceptions. They enable and promote breakthrough thinking and creativity. Oxford University's communities of practice are a prime example of how an institutional environment can promote those interactions that generate knowledge, without compromising the quality and quantity of individual work.

Balancing Interactions with Individual Work

The CoPs model claims that since learning, innovation, and collaboration are social processes, enhancing knowledge creation and sharing in groups can be achieved through social means. That includes all kinds of meetings: staff meetings, lunch breaks, and other social occasions, both formal and informal. Hence the first obvious conclusion of the CoPs model is this: We need to encourage conversations and meetings between people in the organization.

The proper cultural environment begins with a basic organizational value that should be shared by managers and employees. This value relates to the need for everyone to balance their time between personal assignments and networking with others. Whereas every worker needs to fulfill her own assignments and is appraised based on this performance, she must also be allowed and encouraged to network with others. She should have time to discuss ideas, share knowledge, and consult with peers and managers. If implemented properly, this value motivates people to help others with their assignments, thereby promoting mutual learning.

Workers, however, differ in the extent of their willingness to share their knowledge with others. This is why you need to create the proper environment to encourage them to share their knowledge. That is the focus of Chapter 4, on culture. This is also the reason you need to create personal incentives to share knowledge; that is the heart of Chapter 5 on the human focus. But even if you have created incentives and a proper cultural environment, you still have to help employees balance their individual and group demands.

A familiar example for the attainment of this balance comes from the academic world, which is based on a culture of knowledge creation and sharing. The activities of students and professors are aimed at sharing and creating knowledge. Collaborative work, in the form of publishing papers, participating in seminars, and teaching, is encouraged and credited. Researchers keep track of each other's work through visits, seminars, and conferences, supplemented by an informal exchange of written material. These knowledge-sharing activities are balanced with the academic researcher's personal work. The preceding story about Oxford elaborates on how the famous university promotes interactions of knowledge creation and sharing.

In the corporate world, this balance is more difficult to attain. Unlike in academia, CoPs in the corporate world are not always well defined. The checks and balances between personal work and communal work are harder to establish. Many managers do not recognize the importance of formal and informal meetings, and sometimes even despise employees who network because they might be neglecting their own work. This is complicated by the fact that in some cases they are right—some workers do abuse their freedom to interact with others. Thus, if you want to achieve a proper cultural environment, you need to find the right balance between solo time and communal time.

The proper balance is delicate. Figure 6.1 provides a visual representation of the balance needed. Workers who only invest resources in their own assignments, either because they are uncooperative or because management does not allow them, are at the bottom, too solo zone, of the graph. Those who network too much are at the top, too social zone, of the graph. The optimal or right zone is different for each organization, and may vary for different departments of the same organization.

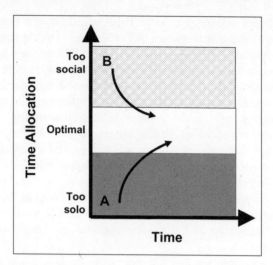

FIGURE 6.1 Time Allocation Vector

Defining the optimal zone, and changing the organization culture over time to attain it along vectors A or B, is no easy managerial task. It requires an understanding of your organization and creative utilization of a repertoire of techniques. But, as we have argued through the CoPs model, it is worth the effort. Nurturing the balance is the key toward creating an organizational culture in which knowledge flows between people and innovation is enhanced.

Having established the social context, and how to reach the right zone, we next describe various forms of interactions.

Extracting Tacit Knowledge—the Corporate Yellow Pages

One of the most common problems in knowledge management is how to find expert help when we have a problem. No matter how trained and experienced our workers are, they cannot know everything. Most of us come across new problems and questions, and the organization has to help us find answers.

One of Tuvya's motivations for studying knowledge management was the case of Ron, a veteran expert whose potential contribution was becoming less and less known to its peers (see Chapter 1). It turns out that many knowledge companies face this problem. When an engineer or scientist encounters a professional obstacle, what does he do? Who does he turn to for professional answers to a problem not encountered before? A similar problem was faced by Monsanto, as described by Bipin Junnarkar, former head of knowledge management at Monsanto:[1]

> *Monsanto, a large chemical manufacturer from St. Louis, has chemical plants that operate 24 hours a day. If there is a problem, someone needs to fix it, and fast, because these urgent problems stop the entire production process. Monsanto struggled with the question of how to guide and expedite the solution of these costly problems. Trying to foresee every kind of problem and writing guidelines for recommended solutions is not possible, as new and unexpected problems will always arise.*

Some managers dream about smart software that will answer all the questions. Well, it is difficult enough to systematically codify the existing, explicit knowledge (we have dedicated Chapter 7 to this problem). To have a prepared written answer to every question that arises, or to codify and anticipate every problem in advance, is impossible.

The most efficient way to solve a novel problem is to ask an expert. The expert transfers her tacit knowledge by giving advice on how to solve it. What the organization can do is to facilitate interactions by making the tacit knowledge available to the appropriate users. The solution that Monsanto and many other companies have found is an organizational directory: a list of experts that identifies their areas of expertise and how to reach them. Since the mid-1990s, for reasons you may guess, almost every organization we know has nicknamed its directory the "Yellow Pages" (and probably nowadays would call it by some variation of a term used on Facebook).

Composing Yellow Pages for the organization is a relatively easy task from an information technology point of view, but a rather challenging task from a cultural point of view. The task involves addressing two cultural issues: (1) How do you identify and choose the experts, and (2) how do you ensure that the experts are available and willing to help in spite of their own busy schedules? Various companies have found different solutions to these problems.

- *Monsanto.*[2] Monsanto assigned "expert roles," whereby being an expert was part of the job description. If you are an expert on something, it is your duty to assist when your expertise is needed. Thus, if there is a crisis in the plant, you are called in to solve it. In Monsanto's solution, the company itself determined who was an expert in each topic.
- *Hoffmann-La Roche.*[3] Hoffmann-La Roche used a sociometric referendum. All the employees were asked to indicate who they turned to for advice when they faced different kinds of problems. They used the

results of this survey to assign the experts in the yellow pages. This method increased the accuracy of the yellow pages, but it also did another thing. By flattering the experts and giving them social recognition, Hoffmann-La Roche gained their willingness to help.

An interesting result of this survey was the discovery of an employee, Rudy, as one of the key sources of knowledge in the company. Rudy was a worker with no official status and recognition. In fact, he was under consideration for layoff because he "did nothing but chitchat."

This story highlights management's potential ignorance of the invisible webs of interactions of knowledge sharing among workers. Sometimes communities of practice are invisible. In this case, crucial tacit knowledge was held by a key figure who was greatly appreciated by his colleagues but underappreciated by his superiors. The management was unaware of his knowledge function until they asked their workers who they turned to as their source of know-how.

- *National Semiconductor.*[4] National Semiconductor used a give-and-take scheme, based on their excellent electronic library. If workers wanted to subscribe to and enjoy the data, they had to indicate what their areas of interest and expertise were. They also had to commit to answering questions about these areas. This method is essentially an exchange of knowledge gifts.

Managers may be disappointed to learn these various solutions, longing for the ultimate method that solves the problem of codifying tacit knowledge once and for all. Moreover, many managers think that their organization is too small to need such a directory. Tuvya was one of those frustrated managers until he was convinced otherwise by what he learned in his own organization:

- *A production department in Rafael.* The manager of one of the production departments at Rafael wanted to create a list of the design and manufacturing experts, who could be called upon to help him solve problems during manufacturing or maintenance. So he put together a directory. He assigned the names according to their functional duty in the organizational structure. The manager in question had never read about company Yellow Pages, but you can probably guess how he also named his directory . . .

Figure 6.2 summarizes the preceding findings. Many organizations with different tacit knowledge problems all arrived at similar conclusions: rather than expecting to codify tacit knowledge, it is wiser to grant the worker the resources and means to interact with the sources of tacit knowledge that are relevant to them. They all use the same brand name of the "Yellow

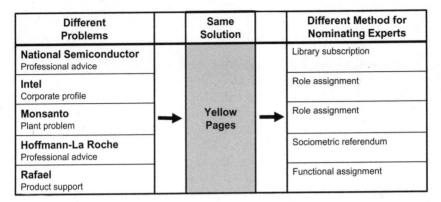

Different Problems		Same Solution		Different Method for Nominating Experts
National Semiconductor Professional advice				Library subscription
Intel Corporate profile				Role assignment
Monsanto Plant problem	➡	**Yellow Pages**	➡	Role assignment
Hoffmann-La Roche Professional advice				Sociometric referendum
Rafael Product support				Functional assignment

FIGURE 6.2 Different Approaches to Creating Company Yellow Pages

Pages" but find different methods to solve the two basic cultural issues of locating and motivating the experts.

Enhancing Interactions in Communities of Practice

Until now, we have discussed ways in which managers can help connect people who are otherwise not connected, in order to foster interactions between them. But, as we have claimed, some of the most important interactions for knowledge creation and sharing occur within communities of practice (CoPs). The next sections discuss how managers can identify, promote, and facilitate various kinds of interactions within communities of practice. The techniques may be structured and formal or, as the following description of Rafael's practices illustrates, they may be semiformal, even fun.

Cake Meetings—Food for Thought for a Section of Knowledge Workers

Most of Rafael's knowledge workers are grouped in units called *sections*, that are both a natural and formal CoP. A typical section, which is a part of the formal organizational structure, consists of about 20 to 40 workers who either share the same professional specialization (such as a section of mechanical engineers and technicians) or belong to the same project. They are usually located in the same geographical area. Such a group is a perfect example of a CoP that would benefit from enhanced interactions.

The section leader is expected to be a professional leader with managerial skills. In addition to his many duties he is supposed to nurture the important interactions within his group. Fortunately, almost all of Rafael's sections have a semi-formal method of interaction called "cake meetings":

Cake Meetings

The weekly sectional cake meetings are based on a long-standing tradition. The origin of the meetings was primarily social: a weekly 60-minute get-together, with rotating responsibility for the refreshments (usually cake, except for the "watermelon meetings" in the hot summer months). Although a social meeting has merit in itself, with time the cake meetings evolved as good section leaders tried to make better use of the time.

Today, beyond announcements and company gossip, cake meetings incorporate descriptions of work in progress, professional lectures, discussions of work methodology, analyses of failures and successes, and other content that is relevant to the section's work. The meetings are long, sometimes more than an hour, but their contribution to the work of the team is substantial. People generally like to participate. They are eager to give presentations, listen to and learn from others, and compete for the "best cake baker" title.

Tuvya has found that these cake meetings are essential for the success of a section. Sections without cake meetings usually have some problems (although, unfortunately, the opposite is not true—just having cake meetings is not enough to guarantee success). The cake meetings evolved naturally into a tradition and were not the result of theory-based interventions. But we know that the reason they work as interactions of knowledge creation and sharing is that they contain the cultural and physical components that promote successful CoPs.

The lesson for managers is that, whether you call them cake meetings, watermelon meetings, happy hour, or any other name, you need to establish a forum for regular meetings with open channels of communication and meaningful work-related content. The needs of the group, organizational culture, and nature of the work will determine the appropriate format of the meetings. The important goal of the format is to simultaneously enable people to talk comfortably and informally while consistently incorporating relevant work-related content.

Cakeless Meetings for Managers

Going up the organizational level, most managers in every organization also participate in a more formal weekly meeting. We do not know how they are called in your organization, but they are usually referred to as a management meeting, staff meeting, or the like. The format may vary, but it usually consists of a subject or two presented for discussion and/or approval, and reporting on current issues or events. Hence the meetings usually have some elements of knowledge sharing and dissemination.

The importance, effectiveness, and attraction of these meeting vary widely. A typical middle manager usually participates in two such meetings: one that he holds for his subordinates and one managed by his superior. (You may guess which meeting he thinks is indispensable and which he complains is a waste of time . . .)

Looking at these meetings from the point of view of CoPs, we may suggest a way to make them more effective. We realize that the participants actually constitute a formal and natural CoP: a team of managers of a specific unit in the organization, or even the general management. We do not recommend turning these meetings into cake meetings: The social purpose is smaller (though it exists) and we also need to keep calorie consumption down. However, we do recommend turning them into knowledge-creating interactions both in style and in content.

Regarding style, there are many techniques to improve the knowledge-creating interactions, some are described elsewhere in this chapter. The common factor is that the chairperson of the meeting should expect and extract members' contributions, and respect different or opposing opinions. A resolution that has been invented by the group is much more likely to be supported than a resolution dictated by the manager, and will usually be on par with or better than the manager's resolution.

Regarding content, we suggest that a large part of these meetings will be dedicated to long-term issues of building intellectual capital. The current and urgent day-to-day issues always require attention. Nevertheless, management must dedicate time to plan and implement the long-term goals in strategy, human resources, customers, processes, and R&D. (All the issues that the Navigator, described in Chapter 2, should mention to us.)

Identifying and Enhancing CoPs

This section describes lessons learned in various organizations about identifying, managing, and enhancing CoPs, while avoiding common problems associated with them.

Can CoPs be Managed? Lessons Learned at National Semiconductor

National Semiconductor (NSC) is an electronics corporation with headquarters in Santa Clara, California. In the late 1990s, motivated by various knowledge-related problems, its top management decided to invest in knowledge management and initiated many activities to enhance CoPs. The following example illustrates how Peter Himes, then director of technology programs in NSC (leader of KM initiatives), described the experience.[5]

NSC discovered that it had several self-organized groups of engineers, from different business units, who had been informally swapping ideas for more than 20 years. Uncovering their contribution made NSC extremely enthusiastic about the idea of CoPs.

They began identifying and promoting other informal CoPs in the organization. They wanted to grant people access to professional experts across the structural boundaries of the organization. The CoPs were encouraged to meet and the practice was touted around the company. At some point they had about 25 such groups.

Unfortunately—although off to a good start—the experiment ultimately failed. Most CoPs endured for a few meetings or a few months and then disbanded. Eventually, only three or four CoPs survived, mostly those that existed before the management initiative.

What happened? Some organizational researchers cite this experiment as proof that CoPs cannot be shaped by management. They must self-organize. But that's a dead-end conclusion—we want to learn from this experiment about what management can do.

Peter Himes had a different explanation. He claimed that the main reason for the failure was that the yield of the meetings was not high enough. It turns out that people were not convinced that they would benefit from contributing to the meetings or that they would gain new knowledge, so it was not worth it for them to invest even the relatively small time needed to participate. Their own assignments gained priority, and the meetings fizzled out. He thinks a similar factor determined the success (or failure) of a series of lectures (see Chapter 7) conducted at that period: Is the added value high enough?

The experience of NSC teaches us several lessons. First, managers must identify existing CoPs, which have added value for both their members and the organization, and help them strive naturally. One of the CoPs that continued to exist in NSC was an informal group of electrical engineers from various departments that meets regularly to discuss problems of electrostatic discharge (ESD). ESD issues affect many electronic designs, which make the group meetings attractive for many engineers.

Second, if you artificially create a CoP which is not a part of the formal structure of the organization, you must ensure continuous added value and benefit to the participants (and their managers and the organization).

Another course of action is to enhance the work of formal groups that are already part of the organizational structure. They often contain characteristics of CoPs, and their interactions can be fostered in the direction of knowledge creation and sharing.

Perhaps the most important lesson, however, is that managers need to make sure that the interactions have meaningful content, thereby providing added value for their members as well as the organization. Interaction forums compete with other demands on workers' time; workers will be motivated to participate only if they see a clear connection between participation and various desired outcomes. In other words, they need incentives to participate, and one major incentive is professional added value. Meetings in which relevant knowledge is not shared and created will be less attractive to participants. Thus, fostering these meetings requires careful consideration of how to promote meaningful content.

Preventing Common Problems with CoPs

Understanding the CoPs model can help managers avoid unnecessary problems when reorganizing the company. Especially, we should be careful not to break existing CoPs. Juanita Brown, a consultant from northern California, shared with us the following chilling story.[6]

A Reengineering That Cuts CoPs

Many companies decided, during the reengineering trend in the early 1990s, that they could dispose of middle management. This was supposed to save them money and flatten the organization structure along the way. Sometimes it worked. But in many cases, companies learned that middle managers held much of the knowledge of the organization, were the core of many CoPs, and served as the brokers of knowledge between CoPs. In these cases, the companies lost more than they gained.

The most dramatic story is about a reorganization in a certain multibillion-dollar global corporation. During a management brainstorming session that Ms. Brown facilitated, the management team realized that in their recent reorganization they had cut almost every formal and informal network! While not immediately affecting financial results, they suffered lots of friction and tension, some slowdown, and definitely less innovation for several months.

Another compelling story regards the restructuring of the Israel Aircraft Industries (IAI). Their KM team describes the experience:[7]

IAI Restructuring and Rebuilding of CoPs

IAI underwent a usual restructuring, aimed at achieving better results through decentralizing the company of 10,000-plus employees into

(continued)

sixteen profit centers. Each sub-company was run independently, and was independently accountable for its financial performance. Some benefits were gained, but also brought forth some problems: the sub-companies often found themselves competing for customers, and the structure inhibited knowledge sharing.

Later, they have moved away from this culture. They are promoting a "one-company" value throughout IAI in order to establish communities of practice that benefit from knowledge sharing. They are attempting to undo the damage of breaking apart existing communities of practice in a new reorganization.

Whether the reorganization is a well-planned step resulting from a thorough analysis of how to improve efficiency and productivity in response to a changing environment, or a response to a managerial trend, management must take care to preserve the existing formal and informal communities of practice.

Indispensable Knowledge-Creating and Knowledge-Sharing Interactions

While promoting the concept of interactions and CoPs, we intentionally did not elaborate on their content, trusting the CoP to define it for itself. However, there are various kinds of special purpose meetings that every knowledge organization must hold. Some examples of such indispensable interactions are described next.

After-Action Review

An important type of knowledge interaction is the after-action review: a professional discussion that analyzes performance with a focus on learning from both successful and unsuccessful aspects. The main focus of the discussion is identifying the gaps between desired and actual performance and drawing conclusions for the next time. The practice has been used by the military for years as a tool for learning from each experience and preventing future mistakes.

In order to be successful, the analysis should be detailed and characterized by openness. Total honesty is a must for after-action reviews to work, but it is not always easily attained. In a proper after-action review, a junior organizational member (in the case of the army, a junior officer; in organizations it may be a recent graduate with limited practical experience) should feel free to criticize more senior colleagues. Inhibitions damage the knowledge gains that result from the process. Thus the climate should focus on giving and receiving feedback rather than evaluation.

It is important that after-action reviews do not become interrogations or investigations. The last thing that promotes openness and candid exchange of lessons learned is a search for someone to blame. People who are preoccupied with defending their decisions and appearing blameless will not contribute to a fruitful analysis of what really went wrong. Only when people feel safe will they volunteer input that may compromise their image.

After-action reviews are an example of a knowledge interaction that goes beyond what the individual can learn alone or in a course. How can you implement the method in your team? Pick a unit of time or performance and institute a periodic review. The review can be of day-to-day tasks at the end of the day, at the end of the week, or at the end of the month. It can follow large projects as well as smaller milestones along the way.

Many claim that reviews should be conducted in groups that include only those people who were involved in the activity itself. It helps the participants feel that they can be totally honest and, more importantly, be committed to the corrective action or corrective action required. Others claim that an outsider, especially if more experienced than the group, is necessary for a better perspective or to make out-of-the-box proposals. In any case, it is important to keep the proper climate in order to minimize status differences and encourage open and honest feedback.

The results of the review should be disseminated to a predetermined target audience in an attractive and user-friendly document. The dissemination of the document constitutes successful lesson learning. The goal of the after-action review is to improve future performance, and this goal is attained if the lessons learned are internalized by those who might repeat the mistakes of their predecessors (or who are supposed to make similar successes). An example of a successful method of dissemination follows.

Failure of the Month

When you conduct after-action reviews, you study what you did and investigate how to do it better next time. One of Rafael's production departments used to publish a "Failure of the Month" newsletter, describing a noteworthy design or production problem and analyzing how to deal with it and/or prevent it. The idea was that if you told everyone about the mistake, they would not repeat it.

(continued)

When Tuvya once visited Hughes Spacecraft and Communications in California, he found that they had a similar practice with almost identical goals and dissemination methods. They, however, used a more positive perspective and called it "lessons learned."

Tuvya told them about Rafael's method, admitting that perhaps because of the Californian "think positive" style, projecting the more constructive title of "lessons learned" was better. So he mentioned that he would suggest that Rafael change the name of their newsletter. But the Hughes people did not agree. They said: "'Failure of the Month' is such a good brand name, do not touch it!"

Peer Reviews

Peer reviews constitute an important set of interactions of knowledge sharing and creation. The idea is that knowledge workers present their work, including work in progress, and receive feedback and ideas from their peers. We are quite familiar with the concept of design reviews (DR), which was born as a contractual requirement of customers in the technical world of engineering projects. It turns out, however, that organizations from other fields, who may have never heard the term *design review*, also use the concept for the same purpose. We believe that peer reviews should be instituted as an integral part of the life of any knowledge organization, so we describe the process in detail here.

EXTERNAL DESIGN REVIEWS IN ENGINEERING PROJECTS Design reviews in engineering projects are performed during predetermined milestones along the life of the project. In each DR, the contractor describes the progress of the project, technical successes and failures, resource utilization, and the plan for the remainder of the project. The customer comments on technical and programming issues and decides whether to continue the program. Design reviews often end up as shows in which the contractor attempts to create a positive impression, since payments often depend on successful progress. In spite of this tendency, DRs often lead to important knowledge gains. A design review entails preparing documentation, reflecting on the progress of the project, sharing knowledge during the presentation, and processing the comments of the customer.

INTERNAL DESIGN REVIEWS IN ENGINEERING PROJECTS Many engineering organizations have learned that in order to be successful they must have internal DRs in addition to the contractual DRs. They establish these reviews as formal steps in the design process and have procedures for conducting them. In these DRs, engineers present their work to peers, superiors, and other experts for a thorough examination. They attend to the recommendations and improve their design accordingly.

Note how these internal DRs are a perfect method for knowledge creation and sharing. The reviewed designers (and designs) benefit from the comments and expertise of the reviewers. The reviewers also gain: They learn about new designs, methods, or problems without working on them directly. Usually, they also gain recognition and prestige as expert reviewers. Internal design reviews are usually official or semiofficial and are supported and even enforced by management. Everybody knows about them, and they attract active participants from outside a small team of designers and reviewers. Employees are motivated to share and accept knowledge with the management's blessing.

The following two examples demonstrate the issue.

Peter Himes on the National Semiconductor Review Experience

When Peter Himes became leader of KM initiatives at NSC, he knew that design reviews were already embedded in the technical culture of the organization. But recognizing their importance, he strove to make them even better. Some of his efforts toward improvement were to encourage cross-departmental participation, whereby participants from other departments were either official reviewers or just sit-ins. Thus he achieved two goals:

1. Increasing the effectiveness of the DRs by incorporating multiple perspectives.
2. Enhancing the informal CoPs by involving everyone in the organization interested in the specific subject.[8]

Tuvya on the Rafael Review Experience

Tuvya witnessed similar success in establishing semiformal internal DRs in his department at Rafael. Initially, some people were reluctant to expose their work to critical review. But as they realized the value of DRs for improving their designs, they began to initiate them with almost no need for management enforcement.

Peer Reviews in Other Organizations

Although the term *design review* is taken from the engineering world, almost every profession has a similar mechanism. For example, as a part of the daily routine in hospitals, department heads walk through patient rooms, accompanied by senior and junior residents and medical students; each patient's doctor describes the case and receives comments from the others. Most advertising agencies have in-house practice sessions before making presentations to customers. Many departments in universities also have regular internal seminars in which colleagues present their current research projects and receive critical feedback.

All in all, peer reviews work. The manager's job is to make sure that such a forum for the exchange of information exists in his unit. This is one of the main messages of the CoPs model. Experience shows that this forum should be established and institutionalized into a coherent format with well-known procedures. It also benefits from incorporating interdisciplinary perspectives.

Methods and Techniques for Effective Interactions

Interactions cannot be managed but they can be facilitated. They can be effectively hosted: The communication environment can be properly designed to enhance deep dialogue—productive conversations for knowledge creation and knowledge sharing. Here we offer some good practices to enhance effective interactions, which you might want to try yourself.

Facilitation of Meetings

The importance of meetings as the arena for knowledge creation and sharing raises a host of considerations. One of the key questions regards who facilitates the meetings. Many professional knowledge managers and organizational consultants suggest that team meetings should not be conducted by the manager. Patricia Seemann of Hoffmann-La Roche tells us the reasons behind this:[9]

> *The managers of a team cannot effectively lead these discussions because they are in power and can be biased. Even though some managers actually want the freedom to speak as "one of the gang," it is difficult for them to remain neutral, and the group does not really expect it. They instead suspect that you are manipulating them.*

Dr. Seemann suggests employing a professional facilitator who is familiar with the subject areas of the team. Being an outsider constitutes, according to her, an advantage for ensuring a proper environment, particularly when you want everyone's participation.

But realistically, it is not practical to have a facilitator at every meeting. Moreover, managers should be careful that the presence and occasional use of a facilitator for important meetings does not prevent the managers from taking upon themselves certain facilitative roles. Managers have an obligation to be active listeners during ongoing interactions and effective leaders of day-to-day meetings. They should make sure they have the skills to extract knowledge from all of their workers on a continuous basis and actively listen and encourage them.

The Physical Environment

Another methodological consideration with respect to managing knowledge interactions is the physical space. The physical environment of a workplace is very important for fostering connectivity and positive interactions between people in a community of practice. However, the physical environment is never a stand-alone issue—it is inherently connected to the cultural environment.

Take the familiar debate between open space and personal offices. Although the ultimate decision may be based on parameters outside of the knowledge context, such as price and flexibility, knowledge management considerations favor open spaces, which encourage people to mingle. But an open-space office alone is not enough to facilitate collaboration and openness—you need to promote the appropriate cultural environment. If the mind-set of the workers is that of an open door, then the physical doors of personal offices will not prevent them from meeting each other. And then you get to keep the main advantage of doors—the option to close them.

Another example is the common practice of conducting important meetings, such as brainstorming sessions about the organization's strategy, outside the regular workplace. Experience shows that these discussions benefit from getting the relevant people together somewhere that is isolated from day-to-day interruptions. Skandia—the Swedish financial services company we mentioned in Chapter 2, and a knowledge management pioneer—fine-tuned this concept to create its Future Center, located on one of the islands in the Stockholm Archipelago, where managers conduct "brain stealing" sessions and generate new ideas about the future.

The Knowledge Café

The knowledge café is a format for meetings especially designed to promote knowledge creation and sharing. It is a method that involves many people at once in a conversation regarding a particular issue that management chooses to discuss. It can be particularly beneficial when management is making a significant decision and is interested in broad input from various perspectives in the organization.

The concept of a knowledge café has several advantages. First, it improves the quality of decisions by incorporating multiple perspectives. Second, the extensive involvement of people fosters a more widespread commitment to the decisions. Also, it is a relatively short process, from a couple of hours to a half-day session, which has significant added value relative to cost.

CAFÉ CONVERSATIONS AT A GLANCE   Having designed strategic conversations for many years, Edna originally questioned the wisdom of using the café method. But when she saw David Marsing, VP at Intel, and David Isaacs, a consultant, coordinate a knowledge café in the first "Knowledge in Action" conference she hosted in Israel in 1996, she fell in love with it right away. The following is a step-by-step outline from TheWorldCafe .com, describing what is involved in these café conversations.[10]

- Seat four or five people at small café-style tables or in conversation clusters. Start up progressive (usually three) rounds of conversation of approximately 20 to 30 minutes each.
- Have the cluster of people at each table engage in questions or issues that genuinely matter to the participants' life, work, or community. Encourage both table hosts and members to write, doodle, and draw key ideas on the tablecloths, or to note key ideas on large index cards or placemats in the center of the group.
- Upon completing the initial round of conversation, ask one person to remain at the table as the host while the others serve as travelers or "ambassadors of meaning." The travelers carry key ideas, themes, and questions into their new conversations.
- Ask the table host to welcome the new guests and briefly share the main ideas, themes, and questions of the initial conversation. Encourage guests to link and connect ideas coming from their previous table conversations—listening carefully and building on each other's contributions.
- By providing opportunities for people to move in several rounds of conversation, ideas, questions, and themes begin to link and connect.
- At the end of the second round, all of the tables or conversation clusters in the room will be cross-pollinated with insights from prior conversations.

- In the third round of conversation, people can return to their home (original) tables to synthesize their discoveries, or they may continue traveling to new tables, leaving the same or a new host at the table. Sometimes a new question that helps deepen the exploration is posed for the third round of conversation.
- After several rounds of conversation, initiate a period of sharing discoveries and insights in a whole-group conversation.

It is in these town meeting–style conversations that patterns can be identified, collective knowledge grows, and possibilities for action emerge. Once you know what you want to achieve and the amount of time you have to work with, you can decide on the appropriate number and length of the conversation rounds, the most effective use of questions, and the most interesting ways to connect and cross-pollinate ideas.

Again, Edna thought some of the results of the café strategy would be problematic. She recognized that a small group would be efficient, but asked how the minds and hearts of so many people could be involved so that the quality of the strategy emerging out of the dialogue would be better and more compelling for future implementation.

At the knowledge café workshop, she saw that the café method worked like magic in achieving both of these goals at the same time and in the same place. It was apparent that one could involve as many people as desired: tens, hundreds, and even thousands! Thus it could really become an energetic happening toward changing strategic implementation, and at the same time be a quality conversation in an intimate setting of small tables exploring opportunities for growth and improvement, as well as any other questions that matter, to solve strategic dilemmas.

Example: Arkia's Strategic Knowledge Café

Israeli airline Arkia (previously discussed in Chapter 3) has used the knowledge café format to gather input for their strategic decision-making.

In one such session, about 150 workers participated from all ranks, seniority levels, areas of operation, and levels of education. Arkia decided to go for maximum diversity in order to bring together as many perspectives as possible, so there were senior managers and junior employees, pilots and flight attendants, marketing people, finance people, and maintenance people, all taking part.

(continued)

> The participants sat in tables of five. In the first round of discussions they raised topics focusing on the future of the company. Each table recorded its discussion on slides, and some presented them in front of everyone.
>
> During the break, the CEO chose the topic of most interest to him from each of the tables' presentations in order to continue the discussion after the break and create a dialogue between the table participants and the CEO.

In this way, the strategic knowledge café can be an effective and efficient method to collect input and raise a consensus of commitment to decisions. Managers attain a perspective that is both broad and intimate within only a few hours. The quality of the decisions rises since the organization simultaneously utilizes the brainpower of many people with different points of view. The commitment of the participants to the decisions also rises, as they feel their input is truly important.

Making the Most of Information Technology

No chapter on knowledge interactions would be complete without a discussion of the role of information technology (IT). IT enables interactions that transmit tacit knowledge, and as such, it is an important knowledge management tool—namely, it broadens the potential number of internal customers for tacit knowledge by making it systematically and broadly available.

Many organizations have information systems designed to support managerial processes, but they are not widely or comprehensively used. Without an organizational culture that encourages knowledge sharing, the information systems will remain unused. There are several ways to promote use of an information system. As we discussed in Chapter 5, concerning the human focus, you can utilize both hard compensation (bonuses, access to other's knowledge and data, promotion) and soft compensation (membership in a knowledge community, establishing a personal reputation among peers). The important point, though, is that having sophisticated technology is not enough—you need to tackle managerial problems in order to encourage and facilitate extensive utilization of the system by employees.

One way in which IT is used to facilitate knowledge interactions is during virtual conferences between people who are working together from various geographical locations. In light of the current trend to reduce air travel, we anticipate that virtual conferencing will increase. It is particularly advantageous in multinational organizations, when limited time resources do not allow face-to-face meetings. Moreover, often when meetings are scheduled, there are too many participants to allow the kind of interactions that promote true knowledge sharing and creation, and there is not enough time to ask all of the relevant questions. A virtual conference, however, allows everyone to ask questions and receive full answers. It is simultaneously more intimate and more time- and cost-effective. Participants contribute and communicate when and where it is most convenient for them.

We have already mentioned, in Chapter 3, IBM Innovation Jam™. This may be the top example of using IT to facilitate knowledge creation and innovation between hundreds of thousands of participants. We shall not elaborate on the tools but on the effect as described in the IBM Jam web site[11]:

IBM Innovation Jam™

Since 2001, IBM has used jams to involve its more than 300,000 employees around the world in far-reaching exploration and problem-solving. ValuesJam in 2003 gave IBM's workforce the opportunity to redefine the core IBM values for the first time in nearly 100 years. During IBM's 2006 Innovation Jam™—the largest IBM online brainstorming session ever held—IBM brought together more than 150,000 people from 104 countries and 67 companies. As a result, 10 new IBM businesses were launched with seed investment totaling $100 million.

Jams are not restricted to business. Their methods, tools, and technology can also be applied to social issues. In 2005, over three days, the Government of Canada, UN-HABITAT, and IBM hosted Habitat Jam. Tens of thousands of participants—from urban specialists, to government leaders, to residents from cities around the world—discussed issues of urban sustainability. Their ideas shaped the agenda for the UN World Urban Forum, held in June 2006. People from 158 countries registered for the jam and shared their ideas for action to improve the environment, health, safety, and quality of life in the world's burgeoning cities.

Note however that most virtual CoPs are much much smaller. There the effectiveness of a virtual interaction, whether in the context of a conference or a straightforward e-mail correspondence, hinges on the formation of a cultural connection and the trust among those involved. An IT-based community of practice is enhanced by familiarity. The familiarity does not have to be face-to-face (it can be promoted, for example, by a closed virtual environment, such as a corporate intranet, granting access only to potentially relevant people), but it is familiarity, openness, and trust that will make utilizing information technology successful. Making the most of IT is more often complicated by the cultural and managerial challenges associated with it than by the technological ones.

Conclusion

Every manager can learn from the examples presented in this chapter and decide what methods of promoting knowledge interactions already exist in his own team. Once these interactions are identified, the next step is to encourage and enhance them. Tuvya underwent exactly this process. He realized at Rafael that they had been promoting knowledge interactions for years, and it was one of the key factors behind its success.

In order to survive, every knowledge organization must have some form of knowledge-sharing meetings. Not having a structured and explicit knowledge management program does not mean that an organization does not offer important knowledge management lessons. It just means that it is not effectively capturing the potential of its interactions. This is why we urge managers to identify the knowledge management practices that are effective in their organization and begin to systematically manage them.

Managing knowledge successfully requires investing in and promoting the appropriate culture and values for encouraging communities of practice. Since communities cannot be forced and sharing tacit knowledge is inherently a voluntary act, the managerial challenge becomes fostering, encouraging, nurturing, and enhancing existing and new interactions within communities. In this way, the manager becomes instrumental in promoting the sharing and creating of knowledge.

While this chapter is on creating knowledge, the next chapter is about capturing existing knowledge, whether for educating new employees or for dissemination throughout the company.

The Magnificent 7

1. Knowledge is created and shared through the social process of interactions.
2. Tacit knowledge can be shared by mentoring and by making experts available through a company's yellow pages.
3. Information systems have great potential for supporting knowledge management if a supportive environment is created.

4. Every knowledge worker should be encouraged to balance his time between his project assignments and networking with others.
5. Managers should encourage the communities of practice (CoPs) that already exist in the organization and foster opportunities for additional interactions.
6. Managers should encourage various forms of knowledge creating meetings, be it "cake meetings," design reviews, after-action reviews or others, and coordinate the physical and social aspects of meetings in order to make them effective.
7. Peer reviews (such as internal design reviews), whereby workers present their work and receive feedback from their peers, constitute an important set of interactions of knowledge sharing and knowledge creation.

CHAPTER 7

Capturing and Reusing Existing Knowledge

In this chapter you will:

Understand that capturing existing knowledge by codifying and disseminating it is a must for knowledge organizations, especially for promoting new use (which prevents unnecessary innovation).

Gain tools for efficient capturing processes and for incorporating them into the ongoing activities of an organization.

Learn how to make the captured knowledge available to all potential knowledge workers, from introducing newcomers to the essential skills to updating the veterans.

Motivation and Obstacles

Capturing existing knowledge, by codifying and disseminating it, is a must for any knowledge organization. It is essential to document the organization's knowledge so that employees can continuously reuse it, as well as find ways for its new-use. *New use* is a term used to describe strategizing new ways of utilizing an organization's knowledge in new and innovative ways.

Often, when introduced to knowledge management (KM) methods, the first bright idea that managers have is to install some kind of fancy software in order to document all the existing knowledge at their disposal and then try to disseminate it. We will later see that this is usually easily said than done.

In addition to documentation, though, there are many other possible methods intended to facilitate the reuse and new use of knowledge. These include practices such as mentoring programs and apprenticeships, workshops, lectures, and continuing education courses through work or in partnership with schools.

And while there are many methods intended to increase reuse and new use, they all have to overcome a similar problem: The process of codifying and disseminating always requires investing extra resources that are almost always scarce—resources like people, time, money, and attention. For this reason, capturing existing knowledge is often neglected even though it directly affects long-term success. The following lesson illustrates this conflict.

A Project Manager's Confession

While at Rafael, David was known not only as a bright scientist and a good project manager, but also as a militant spokesman against the company's "blue reports." These were essentially technical reports in which workers summarized designs, analyses, test results, and other similar work processes.

So why would David object to such a classic method of codifying and documenting technical knowledge? Because they had grown into documents used for purposes other than documentation for knowledge management. Over time, instead, Rafael's promotion system became based partially on the quality and quantity of these blue reports. David claimed that too many reports were written for the sole purpose of securing a promotion and that nobody really needed or read them. What's more, people were wasting time and effort to write them at the expense of their actual projects, thus lowering their productivity and profitability.

After leaving his position at Rafael, David shared some of his impressions of the new job he had recently started while meeting with some of his former colleagues at an event outside of work. "It is much more difficult than I expected," he admitted. "Even though I am now a senior executive, I still need to understand the core technologies, but," he complained, "there are no blue reports there to learn from."

As David's confession to his former coworkers illustrates, the extra effort required to capture the knowledge created during work processes does have an added value. Although the individual worker and his projects may pay a small price in terms of time and energy, the organization as a whole benefits a lot from capturing the knowledge in reports like these.

Of course, some of David's objections were not without validity. While this story is about documentation, there are issues managers should consider when deciding on a method of capturing and disseminating knowledge: documentation, creating lectures, and producing processes for the reuse of knowledge, including mentor programs. In general, some questions managers can ask include:

○ What are the overall benefits of codifying knowledge?

○ What are the particular benefits for users and employees?

○ Is the document worth reading? Is the lecture worth attending? Are the mentor programs robust enough to warrant the time and energy expended?

○ What are the benefits to the organization and its different units?

○ Is any particular method of capturing and disseminating knowledge more efficient than another? Are the methods efficient enough?

Managers also need to weigh things like conflicts that arise when specific units or projects are more burdened than others, or than the company as a whole, in terms of documenting knowledge. They also need to think about the methods of implementation, like whether a different modern IT solution might be more suitable than a classic reporting style, and so on.

Overall, what is needed is an efficient method of capturing knowledge, an effective way to make this knowledge available to all potential users, and a fair way to share the expense (in both time and money). In this chapter, we supply examples of the various techniques for installing proper documentation and dissemination processes in an organization.

Documenting Knowledge Efficiently

Documenting and codifying existing knowledge is usually a prerequisite for capturing the knowledge for future sharing and new use or reuse. In addition, it is often a must, required for manufacturing the end product or by regulatory agencies. However, as previously demonstrated by David's example, it should be done in an efficient way with as little interference with ongoing work as possible. This section describes some methods to respond to this challenge.

Example: The Pharmaceutical Industry

Documents are a large part of the work process at pharmaceutical companies, particularly while developing a new drug. Although the end customer is the individual patient, the actual customer during the development phase is the FDA, which regulates the introduction of new drugs into the marketplace. The lengthy process of new drug approval (or NDA) is based on documents presented to the FDA. So effective documentation of the processes of companies in this industry is critical, and may have strategic implications.

The following example outlines the documentation methods established at Hoffmann-La Roche Pharmaceuticals in the 1990s. It is presented by Patricia Seemann, who at that time was their director of knowledge systems:[1]

Hoffmann-La Roche's Knowledge Map

Managers at Hoffmann-La Roche decided to focus KM initiatives on accelerating the documentation required for the NDA process. They forecasted that saving just one day's work by efficiently documenting certain processes could be worth up to $1 million for the company per product. Over three months, that translates to a savings of approximately $90 million per product, and there were about 30 products that Hoffmann-La Roche wanted to document simultaneously!

They began by evaluating the quality of the documentation methods, and it turned out they were not effective enough. Some of their main findings were as follows:

- The documents were not customer-friendly. People in the drug development groups wrote lengthy documents for themselves but they were not appropriate to the needs of the FDA's customers.
- Overall, the knowledge that needed to be documented was not easily available or retrievable. It was difficult and time-consuming to assemble the information from all the various departments.
- Similarly, overall, the knowledge was not shared. The same questions had been surfacing back to the FDA over the course of many years, but each new project was always surprised by them because their existence was not known outside of the group in which they originally surfaced.

The Hoffmann-La Roche managers took some steps to redefine the process of presenting knowledge documentation. The first step was to create a template document to satisfy the customer. Working together with an array of ex-regulators, they realized that regulators typically have three crucial questions about a drug:

- Is it safe?
- Does it work?
- Does it work well/sufficiently?

From these top questions, they then drilled down to more detailed guidelines to create more extensive documentation, including additional specific questions and more templates for the capturing of the information.

The next step was to create a *knowledge map*. The knowledge map included the detailed templates, various links to directories of information and findings, as well as the names of people who had the answers to particular questions. It also documented examples of the experience gained from all previous projects.

Hoffmann-La Roche's process is a classic example because it addresses a slew of the requirements necessary for proper documentation. It is a process organized in reaction to the specific needs and questions of its customers, and it directly benefits the producing organization and its individual workers by creating long-term gains for the company and its users.

Even though the cost of implementing the program was several million dollars, management was ready to pay because the expected gain was very high.

Example: The Aerospace Industry

Documentation in the aerospace industry is as important as in the pharmaceutical industry, but for somewhat different reasons. The aerospace industry is a long-term, technology-driven industry, conducting research and development for sophisticated products, with product cycles of 10 years and longer. For these companies, product development, maintenance, and support take many years. Communication of knowledge and certain work processes is essential to the success of the company in keeping track of the organization's experiences. They need documentation to develop, produce, and support current products, as well as to develop future ones.

The level of investment and sophistication in documentation is different for each phase of a product's life cycle, according to the perceived benefit. In the *production and maintenance phases*, documentation is a must. The need and benefits in these departments are obvious, so their documentation practices are very advanced and continuously improving with time. Each company selects one of the commercially available information technology (IT) solutions, and requires employees to use it.

The documentation in these departments is an extensive discipline in itself, and we do not elaborate on it here. We do want to mention just one family of software these companies use, called product data management (PDM) software. It contains, organizes, and updates all the data necessary for the manufacturing of a product: thousands of drawings and assembly instructions for all of a product's components, from items and parts to subassemblies and then full products. We mention it because it may be also used during the development phase, as we discuss later.

The efficiency of documentation during the *development phase* of products is not as obvious an issue for companies as during the production and maintenance phases. However, tackling it is a must for an efficient development process and good engineering practice, which eventually does help improve the bottom line.

The example that follows describes an experience at Rafael, which demonstrates the problem of knowledge documentation and the way the solution is advancing with time. Earlier in this chapter, we discussed the blue reports at Rafael and how they were consuming too much time and effort for today's fast-paced age (versus when they were first developed). The following example describes another old-time method, the *development folder*, and how in order to retain its benefits it needs to be paired with modern IT.

The Development Folder

When Tuvya was a young engineer at Rafael, he was invited to a lecture on why and how to prepare and use a development folder. The lecturer, Giroa Shalgy, was a young junior engineer at the time (but later became a CEO). The message of his talk was to keep a continuous daily log of all the activities associated with a project. The log included information on the data, calculations, and test results of a project, as well as the design considerations. The development folder could be a personal folder but could also be shared with colleagues working on the same project.

Mr. Shalgy spoke about how the incremental documentation process, done by an individual as a project is happening, is faster and more reliable and accurate than when a report was written at the end of a project. It is also a much less tedious and daunting task. Thus, the development folder process also relieved the burdens associated with the blue reports discussed previously, while keeping most of their knowledge management benefits.

Tuvya liked the idea of incremental documentation and has been using it ever since when doing engineering design work. He later discovered that similar methods were used in competitive aerospace companies, only the processes had different names: For instance, when Tuvya was introduced by Arian Ward to some Hughes engineers in

1997, they were using what they called a "project book" for the same purpose.[2] Later, when Tuvya described the idea to Professor Bryson, an internationally known veteran leader in aerospace sciences from Stanford University, the professor recalled using a similar "workbook" in his days as a young engineer at Raytheon in the 1950s!

While using the development folder idea, there are a few things we should keep in mind:

- The process takes self-discipline. It must be done properly, in a timely manner, and in an orderly format.
- The development folder can lack the extra insight gained in writing a report at the end of a process. However, if in the end an employee wants to or has to write an official report, he can do so by copying most of it from the folder he's kept all along.
- If you have handwriting like Tuvya's, the development folder might not be as suitable a tool for knowledge sharing as you'd hope!

All kidding aside, modern developments in the methods of documenting processes, and pairing them with modern IT capabilities, enable a wider and more convenient use of this idea of the development folder method. For instance, we may use the PDM software, aimed initially just for production purposes, to include different sets of development data like R&D data, information for the subassemblies in relation to the whole system, and other considerations as a project develops. The PDM coupled with modern IT software enables updating throughout the full life cycle of a project and makes for easier knowledge sharing.

Some modern developments include:

- Creating computerized templates that can be used to structure what data should be preserved and how to write it up.
- Collating information from design reviews, which now influence the whole design process, and having it automatically download into the development folder.
- Getting other information, like calculations from specialized design software, test summaries, and so forth, also easily added by cut-and-paste or special download.

This modern realization of the development folder, combining the old method with new capabilities, satisfies most current requirements for efficient documentation of R&D. The benefit for capturing various user and organizational processes is obvious, and there is almost no extra effort beyond what was already required in the usual process of design and manufacturing. Of course, one condition still exists: It still requires self-discipline.

While the preceding examples come from experience gained in the aerospace industry, most professions can use a similar combination of this self-documentation process and pair it with any number of basic software systems available today. They may be as simple and general as word processing and/or spreadsheets, or systems that are more customized to a particular profession.

IT—Has the Future Already Arrived?

Throughout this book we try to emphasize the cultural sides of KM, fighting the notion that KM is about fancy Information Technology (IT) software to document existing knowledge. However, modern developments in the late 2000s and early 2010s may suggest a better solution for both cultural and technical issues.

These prospects are demonstrated in the story of Eran, Tuvya's young next-door neighbor, who has recently graduated as an engineer and recruited to the military into a technical unit:

The Younger Guys Solve an Old KM Problem

Eran's technical unit is responsible for developing and maintaining some electronic equipment. This unit suffers from various severe sources of KM problems:

- They have to support legacy equipment, aging 10 or even 20 years, versus few years in commercial electronics.
- They are not only maintaining the equipment, but they are also responsible for defining new equipment and overseeing its development and production.
- The staff consists mainly of very young and inexperienced engineers and junior managers, like Eran. They change frequently, with a typical assignment of about two years. This, combined with very heavy workloads, prevents them from achieving deep knowledge of the old equipment or gain familiarity with the process of developing new ones.

Hence there is a large problem of knowledge capturing and dissemination. Legacy knowledge is distributed in many outdated paper documents or even computer documents, difficult to browse and maintain. Some knowledge is only in people's heads, where some of them are older veterans who are only available for short-term reserve duty.

The problem existed for many years, and solutions seemed either impractical or too expensive. Eran, together with some other new young engineers, suggested a solution based on a Wiki-style platform. They have been acquainted with such platforms since high school, and know they offer a convenient way to accumulate, access, and update data.

Initially senior managers, the unit commanders, did not like this idea. They were especially worried about configuration control and content control. And they have some reasons to worry—these are the same reservations raised against the famous global Wikipedia concept.

However, the young guys decided that something is better than nothing. They prepared the tool nevertheless, and succeeded in making it useful and achieving extensive usage. They later introduced some configuration control methods, thus eventually convincing their junior managers and later even their senior managers.

The moral of the story has several aspects:

- First, it has the elements of grass root initiative, which many times arrives at more acceptable solutions then methods dictated from above.
- Second, the solution is a good example of a simple and inexpensive tool, which is very convenient and easy to use and is not a burden on employees' time. Thus it fulfills all the requirements we stated at the beginning of this chapter for an efficient method of knowledge capturing and dissemination tool. It can also easily be used as a modern realization of the development folder.
- Third, and maybe most important as a hope for the future, this tool may overcome some cultural obstacle: People like it, use it frequently, and are encouraged to share their knowledge with others.

Teaching the Organization What It Knows

In this next section, we discuss an array of methods available to employees for capturing and disseminating the knowledge that already exists within their organization. The methods are ordered from one-to-one mentoring to one-on-many encounters like lectures. Further, the various types of one-on-many encounters are ordered by increasing commitment from the employees and organization, from sporadic lectures to continuing education in courses and internal schools.

Mentoring and Apprenticeships

The basic interaction for disseminating tacit knowledge is a dyadic, or one-on-one, situation. The best example is apprenticeship or mentoring, in which newcomers to a job learn the ropes of their new role. Mentoring is appropriate in many contexts, from the guilds of the Middle Ages to modern-day training of doctors and professors.

In these familiar cases the potential benefits for both trainer and trainee are obvious. However, in other cases, the benefits are not as easily realized. Hence we need mentoring programs to formalize the process, thus ensuring that the mentor facilitates the processing of insights and does not abandon the learner. Organizations with very different characteristics and types of knowledge all face the same problems, and the examples in this section show how they have been resolved.

The Supermarket Cashier

A simple but instructive case regarding mentoring was revealed to Tuvya during a casual talk with a cashier in his local supermarket. Tuvya always tries to choose a particular cashier's line because she handles customers very efficiently and with a smile. One day the cashier proudly introduced Tuvya to her new colleague at the next cash register, and boasted how she taught her all the secrets of the trade (i.e., everything she knew).

Such a classic example of apprenticeship is probably common in supermarkets, so it is no wonder the cashier's management instructed her to dedicate valuable time for teaching the new cashier the ropes. In this case, management not only chose a good mentor, but also increased the potential success of the training by tasking the cashier with the training. Tasking her with the training actually gave her extra motivation because she felt pride at being senior enough to instruct others!

LEARNING THROUGH EXPERIENCE   The following examples describe how knowledge workers (KWs) should aspire to learn continuously throughout their careers by learning directly from experience as well as from others' experience.

A BALANCE OF ATTENTION IS KEY TO QUALITY MENTORING   Rafael has a structured and formal apprenticeship program. Each new employee, be it a

The Bank Teller and the Consultant

Historically, banks in Israel have trained new employees by sending them to an off-site job training to be tellers. At some point they decided to switch the order. They had new recruits first serve as tellers for six months, with mentors by their side, and only afterward sent them to the training. They realized that this was a more effective method for knowledge dissemination than simply sending them to the training right away.

Seeing the success of this method, Edna's consulting firm also applies this concept in its practice. In general, she prefers to hire BA-level workers to MBAs because they are encouraged to work and study for their master's degree simultaneously. Overall, Edna sees this as a win-win for both her firm and the new employees because the latter benefit from the combination of studying while directly applying their education to their daily work office experiences.

secretary, a production worker, an engineer, or a scientist, is assigned a mentor. In the program, the mentor prepares a customized mentoring curriculum for the newcomer, which is checked and approved by the department manager. It almost always consists of on-the-job training, where the newcomer is performing tasks with the help of the mentor.

The program is especially comprehensive for engineers. It ensures that new engineers learn all about the different aspects of the work environment during the first year of work. It particularly emphasizes the specific subjects not taught in the university: working with specific trade software and gaining valuable experience in collaborating with coworkers inside and outside company departments. The mentor refers the newcomer to various sources of information and also contributes his own tacit knowledge.

The mentoring program at Rafael is subject to formal reviews. The progress of every newcomer is checked at least quarterly by the department manager. One division even instituted a yearly meeting of the participants in the mentoring program, involving both mentors and trainers and the division head, in order to provide feedback on the process.

In rare cases there are problems with the mentoring process. Usually it comes down to a bad match of personalities, solved by replacing either the mentor or the newcomer and reassigning the couple. The opposite problem is even rarer, but amusing to watch. For example, in some departments we have found mentors—usually older veterans—behaving like an overly worried parent and becoming protective of their apprentices. These mentors enthusiastically give their best to the newcomers, investing lots of time and effort to teach them everything. However, this kind of attention can also make the trainees insecure, feeling like they can't work unsupervised, let alone manage others. In most of these cases, though, mentoring yielded positive results, and efforts to step in and correct the overly attentive mentoring were successful.

Overall, because the apprenticeship program at Rafael has brought about such success for the parties involved, it is now an essential part of managing knowledge workers at Rafael. New employees usually praise the program and appreciate the knowledge gained.

The mentors sometimes do complain about the amount of time they spend on this activity in terms of balancing it with their day-to-day tasks. However, they usually enjoy it and understand its importance. They are further motivated by the newcomer taking on some of their projects in the spirit of training, and by management's praise in giving them credit as experts tasked with passing on their expertise to newcomers.

Lectures and Workshops

When managers are first introduced to the issues of knowledge management and the methods for solving them, their second bright idea is usually scheduling lectures or workshops. (Remember, as mentioned in the beginning of the chapter, the first bright idea is adopting an IT solution for documenting knowledge.) They usually think of the various experts, from inside and outside the organization, whom they can invite to share their experience on relevant subjects. Some managers even succeed in launching a weekly, biweekly, or monthly series of expert lectures. However, after the initial buzz of the programs, most of them fizzle out after a few events.

When we look at the reasons why so many are tempted to launch a series of lectures, we see that they are really a useful method for disseminating knowledge. First, they are one-on-many encounters, which are more efficient for some subjects when compared with the one-on-one training of mentoring. And when the lecturer is from inside the organization, we see the additional benefit of codifying existing knowledge from within the company.

The reason lecture series eventually fail to gain popularity is that they take time away from a knowledge worker's other work commitments. It is especially difficult when attending the lectures requires the KW to be in a specific place on a specific date and time. If the lectures are not of the utmost importance, they are seen as a nice bonus but not a requirement, and the lecture loses the competition for the workers' time.

HOW TO MAKE A LECTURE OR WORKSHOP SUCCEED   Contrary to those unsatisfactory experiences, there are examples where some lectures did better than others. National Semiconductor Corporation, for instance, experimented in the 1990s with various KM initiatives like biweekly lectures and technical seminars and they cite them as very successful. From their headquarters in Santa Clara, California, they coordinated lecture series for several years with continually large audiences (with an average attendance of about 15 percent of their employees showing up).

Peter Himes, who at that time was responsible for some of the lecture initiatives at NSC, says the following things helped to make the lectures a success:[3]

- *Offering valuable and unique content.* The lectures at NSC were usually given by an internal expert who provided some added value on a subject beyond what is commonly known or written in textbooks. For example, a veteran analog design engineer might explain how one "really" designs an analog circuit in the NSC environment.

- *Conducting lectures in an interactive format.* Only half of the allotted lecture time was dedicated to the formal lecture. The rest of the time was dedicated to a question-and-answer session where both group and one-on-one conversations occurred during the break.

- *Making sure the subject is relevant.* The subject of the lecture should be potentially interesting for a large enough target audience to justify the effort and create the most social interest.

- *Providing a professional preparation.* NSC designated staff for organizing the lectures and helping the lecturers prepare for them.

These elements ensured that employees would benefit. They were eager to participate in peer lectures, on relevant issues, tailored to fit their knowledge needs.

Many people might naturally consider these factors essential to any good lecture series. However, in the workplace environment and for the purpose of attaining proper KM, the most important aspects to include would be codifying in-house knowledge and motivating coworkers to attend and learn from it.

THE ALTERNATIVE APPROACH   In addition to using NSC's guidelines for good lectures, you may want to avoid classrooms and replace larger settings with some kind of personalized learning. The simplest method is through a company intranet: E-mailing written material or presentations, which the worker can read in his room and when he has the time, will enhance the experience. This way KWs retain the advantages of having an expert codify existing knowledge for them, but they can use it at their convenience. The current NSC web site links to a realization of the above: Analog University®, offering on-demand videos and webinars in the Knowledge Exchange Center.[4]

Another method is to group disconnected lectures into some kind of structured course, which we explain in the next section.

Courses

Courses may have a unique and important role in capturing and disseminating knowledge. The structure of a course in an organization is somewhat similar to a course at a university. It consists of a series of related lectures, about a specific connecting subject, for the same continuing audience. They involve many hours that may be spread over a period of weeks or months. Some courses may be taught by an outside expert or vendor, such as a course in a computer language; others are prepared in-house for teaching special skills.

Courses entail a larger commitment of time than sporadic lectures, and therefore larger efforts, but hopefully with larger gains. The following example shows how courses became a major turning point in a department at Rafael.

Renewing an Electronic Integration Section

In 2006, Yael was a newly appointed manager of an electronic department at one of Rafael's divisions. Right away, she identified the problems in the electronic integration section of her department as a major crisis, requiring immediate and extensive action.

This section was responsible for the design and testing of the electronic interface between various components of an aerospace vehicle. The processes occurring in that section are not usually taught in a university setting, and they are almost always interdisciplinary: requiring not only knowledge of electronics, but also knowledge on how specific components work, the interfaces between them, and the requirements from the system as a whole in terms of performance, reliability, safety, and so on.

The crisis Yael reported had many facets. In the past, this used to be an elite section that grew many senior project managers. However, for various reasons the section had decayed and was perceived as a lower-level section in the company, both by its internal clients and by its workers. Clients were constantly complaining about the work from that section.

Yael quickly took many steps to upgrade the department, including appointing new managers and hiring more qualified engineers. But a major step in its transformation was realizing that there was no structured body of knowledge common to the whole section. Every group of workers used different unwritten methods and all groups were lacking some basic skills, especially because they were not sharing their knowledge.

Yael decided to establish a comprehensive course on integration. She appointed one of the section experts to design a course and manage it. The curriculum included lots of lectures on relevant systems and components by the organization's top experts for each subject, as well as special lectures on integrating methods from different areas. A very important outcome of the preparation of this course was the creation of a unified integration method, based on the knowledge assembled from the experts and the various groups of that section.

The course consisted of weekly half-day sessions, continuing for almost a year. Half the section members were chosen to participate in the first round and, at the same time, continue fulfilling their commitment to their projects. In spite of the burden of working on both, the course was completed on time and very few participants were forced to drop out.

The result of these steps was a visible revitalization of the section. Over time, instead of low-level assignments, its workers became responsible for important designs. The unified integration method not only affects this section but also improves the way and pace that products across many departments are assembled and tested, thus leading to increased satisfaction for both clients and workers.

The course at Rafael is a very good example of proper knowledge management. The process of capturing knowledge and disseminating it was very successfully *managed*. Any obstacles to success were carefully removed to assure benefits for everyone involved.

The benefits to the organization were obvious. The process of revitalizing the department was welcomed by senior management. Project leaders and managers alike did not complain about workers putting time and energy into the process, and especially in the course, because they knew the long-term benefits were worth it.

The benefits to the students of the courses were also obvious. The material was important and interesting, and they understood that the course was a positive step for their career path.

Relating this example to some issues discussed before, we see that:
- Such a course, in spite of its being a major effort for the organization, is definitely more efficient than sporadic lectures or one-on-one mentoring.
- The course engaged lecturers in knowledge capturing, as the students experienced knowledge dissemination and sharing.

■ As the two interactions combined, the stage was set for the creation of new knowledge, culminating in the preparation of a new, unified method for electronic integration.

Internal Schools for Continuing Education

Some companies establish an internal school to teach their employees company procedures. In its simplest form, a school may be just a collection of courses—a professional training department with a mission to help other departments organize in-house or off-site courses like the ones described in the previous section. A school may also be responsible for cross-organization courses, like management or strategy courses. The school can also create and share knowledge about how to implement successful courses.

For many major corporations, the internal school is more than a collection of courses. It can be a symbol of the common culture and knowledge that unites an organization. In these cases, the school is usually called a university or academy, and its goal is to assure an efficient and unified dissemination of knowledge required for both low-level and high-level workers. It teaches employees specific procedures, methodologies, and competencies needed for their work. The school focuses on teaching those things that the employees need to know for the job that they did not learn during their formal education. Some examples include:

■ *The military.* In every country, the military has schools that teach specific job knowledge that soldiers cannot learn from a regular high school or university education alone. However, the schools and their course offerings differ widely from country to country, and even between various forces of the military organization in the same country.

■ *Corporate cultures.* McDonald's "Hamburger University" and Disney's "Disney University" are just two of the most commonly known examples, with training programs catering to teaching their employees skills they will need on the job.

■ *Niche industries.* Amdocs, a multinational Israeli software provider, has a school where workers learn the basics inherent to the niche Amdocs organization: its marketing methods, proposals writing, and so on.

Once an organization has documented its knowledge processes and shared its knowledge in various ways, it is poised to be able to reuse and create new uses for it.

Reuse and New Use

In some people's experience, the term *reuse* can be associated with stifled creativity, but we think an appropriate way of looking at knowledge reuse is in terms of *new use*. Using existing knowledge in new, creative ways is essentially engaging in efficient innovation. It is about building on the accomplishments of predecessors and accumulated knowledge in an organization, rather than starting from scratch each time you embark on the design of a new product or process.

The following examples clearly demonstrate the way some organizations are solving common reuse problems, and also convey the kinds of atmosphere in which organizations are reusing knowledge and innovating.

Example: Reuse at Hughes

Hughes (now Boeing SDC)*, a leading satellite manufacturer, is about reuse. Satellites are so expensive and prone to failures in the harsh environment of space that designers must use proven components. An expert in the industry describes this paradox with the adage, "No new component will fly on a satellite unless it has already flown before."

The methods of reuse at Hughes were discussed in a meeting in the late 1990s with their KM director at that time together with two team leaders in the engineering group. They described:[5]

> *At Hughes, the most successful designs of new satellites utilize elements from previous designs. The company provides engineers with data on previous products and components, so they avoid unnecessary risks and make the most of resources so they are not reinventing existing knowledge.*

> *When asked if they are not bored by working on old stuff, they claimed the opposite. They do not need to reinvent the old stuff and work hard on the simple repetitive tasks, but to concentrate on innovation in the important new things and especially the system for a new mission.*

The database at work at Hughes was a major sponsored project in documentation. Readers with an engineering background will appreciate the effort it took for Hughes to create such a database, because product design in engineering is usually not a simple plug-and-play. You cannot reuse a component unless you have enough knowledge on its design. You not only need its current characteristics and performance statistics, but also

---

*Hughes was acquired by Boeing in 2000 to become Boeing Satellite Development Center (SDC).

its full design history, the context of its design, the data on testing it and especially its failures, and so on. And even then, there are plenty of examples of failures in the reuse programs.

Therefore, from a KM perspective, the experience at Hughes has been a source of motivation in the field of reuse and new-use. Reusing proven components increases communality, thus lowering expenses and increasing reliability. The new-using of old components does not stifle innovation; on the contrary, engineers focus on innovation by optimizing the system, based on the reused components, for a new mission.

Example: New Use at Intel

We mentioned in Chapter 4 that Intel has the slogan "Copy Exactly." In the context of reuse and new use we can look at this slogan from another perspective.

When Tuvya first heard this slogan in the late 1990s from an Intel Fellow in California,[6] the meaning seemed simple and obvious: When it comes to producing chips in different locations, the slogan emphasizes that it is very, very important for Intel to make sure that all its fabrication plants worldwide produce its chips in exactly the same way. Thus the customer always has the same product, and when a problem is discovered and fixed in one plant, it can be fixed in all the plants in the same way.

In terms of reuse, a simple lesson to take away may be that innovation toward new use does not always belong in every work process, every organizational setting, or every production plant. While Intel is famous for its innovation in developing chips, at its production level copying exactly was a slogan to succeed by.

About 10 years later Tuvya learned a more sophisticated lesson during a visit to Intel FAB in Israel and attending a presentation by the manager of Intel Israel.[7] Actually, the production plant does have many new uses and innovations. Of course, the recipe of making the chip is still required to be "copy exactly" reuse of knowledge. However, all other activities associated with production, from the design of the impressive FAB to managing its day-to-day operation, involve major and continuing innovations.

Conclusion

This chapter described the various methods of capturing the knowledge that already exists in an organization and disseminating it to all relevant parties. It complements the previous chapter about creating new knowledge.

While this chapter was about inside knowledge, the next chapter will look outside the organization: the important knowledge that we gain from customers.

The Magnificent 7

1. Knowledge organizations must capture the knowledge of their workers.
2. The knowledge that is captured should be valuable to a complete array of potential users and continuously updated.
3. Knowledge-capturing processes should be efficient so that they do not require too much time from employees. Providing employees with templates or fostering incremental documentation processes can enhance the efficiency of the knowledge-capturing process.
4. Organizations should provide incentives to their knowledge workers for documenting their knowledge to share with others.
5. Current (early 2010s) IT solutions make knowledge capturing and dissemination not only more efficient but also help to alleviate some cultural obstacles.
6. Methods with some elements of continuing education, such as mentoring, courses, and intranet services, are effective combinations of capturing and disseminating knowledge in organizations (and they are usually preferred to sporadic events like lectures).
7. New use of captured knowledge should be encouraged in order to create an accumulation of knowledge and prevent unnecessary innovation.

CHAPTER 8

The Customer Focus

Harnessing Customer Knowledge through Meaningful Interactions

In this chapter you will:

Learn about the importance of constant contact with customers for continuous knowledge creation on all organizational levels.

Gain tools that enable you to glean important knowledge from your customers and make them partners in the process of innovation.

Imagine an organization that conducts customer satisfaction surveys and bases its view of them on the statistical analysis of the surveys. Sound familiar? Now imagine a change in tactic. Imagine the organization invites its customers to an interactive meeting. The customers arrive, spend a few hours, eat a snack, and share their knowledge with the organization coordinating the event.

There's quite a difference between the two scenarios because the interactive meeting is much more personal and immediate. Why spend time, effort, and money on a survey when so many customers are willing to tell you what they think for free?

It is a simple fact that people seem to enjoy being asked what they think, feel, and expect. All you have to do is invite your customers to a conversation, ask some questions, and, most importantly, listen. Then you will discover how valuable direct communication is in creating your future with them. By helping the organizations that supply them with the products and services they need, they are also helping themselves. It's a mutually beneficial situation where both sides win. In this chapter, we discuss ways in which you can create value by interacting more closely with customers.

Customers Are Willing to Share What They Know

Knowledge management inevitably involves making customers partners in shaping an organization's future. Customers generally want to be partners with organizations they do business with, and they are willing to share the various types of knowledge they possess.

The following example demonstrates the importance and benefits of such interactions.

The Furniture Company Knowledge Café with Customers

Several years ago Edna consulted with a well-established Israeli furniture manufacturing company. During their talks, it became obvious to Edna that the company managers did not realize how much relevant knowledge their customers held and that they could easily get to it by conversing with them in order to use it for both their benefits.

As part of her consulting, Edna suggested the furniture company set up knowledge cafés with two of their most strategic customer bases—architects and carpenters. The management team was apprehensive in coordinating the event. They wondered if any of the customers would show up, among other things. But to their surprise, they did.

A number of leading architects from Israel showed up for the first knowledge café. They were not paid for attending; they were just offered coffee and cake and arrived ready to fill in questionnaires, after which they gladly engaged in a conversation on "questions that matter." They focused on products, including why some of them, though beautifully packaged and practical, were no longer trendy. They discussed how some products sold little while other product solutions, even when less practical and more expensive, were more popular. Since the architects were opinion leaders in the field—they told the end customer what to buy—their opinions were highly informative.

During the café, the organizers and the participants found a typical KM problem was surfacing. When the café was complete, the company realized the customers were not disinterested in their products, but were simply not aware that the company was manufacturing newer products with beautiful colors and textures.

Further, similar feedback was captured from the second knowledge café organized for the carpenters. In the end, working directly with their customers (the opinion leaders of their specific market) resulted in a significant growth in income for the company.

Whenever Edna encounters skeptical and reluctant organizations, she relays the outcomes of this story about how intensive knowledge sharing with customers can lead to dramatic results. It is sometimes ironic that companies are willing to spend a lot of money on market research, while they ignore the great opportunity of just talking to their own customers in a relaxed setting. Edna likes to ask CEOs when they last had a long conversation with one of their customers to find out about the customer experience (what customers need and expect), in order to decode what would most interest them, even before they know it themselves.

Surveys versus Direct Communication

The 1980s was an age of quality revolution. Everyone in business was excited about deepening their partnership with customers, knowing that their customers were a key component of their future success. But our experience in consulting with companies during that time did not indicate that the partnerships organizations had with their customers were real partnerships. We saw organizations overly employing customer satisfaction surveys and relying too heavily on statistics. In these types of communications, the customer remains anonymous. Even though they thought they were connecting with their customers, companies employing these types of methods were not really engaging in a dialogue with them.

Overall, we think that some of the market surveys are a waste of time and money. They bring organizations to conclusions about future demands on their resources based on hypothetical questions. We believe it is much more preferable to interview one's current loyal customers directly—to really talk to them and see how they think. The direct conversation should not be about solving day-to-day problems per se, but about making the customer a partner in shaping the future of an organization. Asking your customers questions such as:

- Which core competencies should we develop?
- Which new markets should we enter?
- What type of services do you really need?
- How can we connect to your real needs?

At Supersol, the largest chain of supermarkets in Israel, management experimented with certain methods of direct communication with customers by installing local customer advisory boards in each of their stores. These customers advised store management on where and how to display products as well as what type of services they needed versus which ones were a waste of time. What a unique and inexpensive consulting team!

The Living Lab Concept

An innovative and relatively new method where customers and users are seen as full partners in the development of new products is known as a *Living Lab*. A Living Lab is a new product development (NPD) project team, which not only includes the developers but also incorporates the end users from the very beginning as full team members.

This is very different from the usual procedure: analyzing the needs of end users, then doing R&D with developers only, and evaluating the almost-ready product with the end users only in the last stages. When end users become developers themselves, the project becomes a Living Lab, since it allows for ongoing improvement of the new product through an ongoing fine tuning based on constant end-user feedback.

An example of such a project developed in a Living Lab in which Edna and her team have been involved is the wearable computer, wearIT@work:[1]

The Wearable Computer

Edna's team was a full partner in a big European Union consortium which developed systems of wearable computers for a variety of working environments: health care, production, maintenance, and emergency response. The end users—physicians, production workers, maintenance engineers, and firefighters—were full members of the project team from the very beginning. They helped design the prototypes, they tried them, and they offered new perspectives and new solutions throughout the process which the hardware and software developers had not thought about.

Edna's team, as a partner in this project, was responsible for the social science research piece in it. At the very end of the project, in interviews they did with the product developers from hardware and software, they asked what surprised them during the project. They were fascinated to find out that the largest surprise was the complexity of the customers—not just the end users but the whole ecosystem of users and decision makers. They had not accounted for it!

This proves the importance of the Living Lab concept, in which a user-centered design team allows for the use of customer knowledge in a very intensive way.

Learning from Internal Customers

While this chapter is mainly dedicated to the *external* customer, we use this section to mention the too-often-overlooked knowledge management of *internal* customers. Edna is constantly amazed at how organizations neglect to take a good look within and "know what they know."

Typically, information technology (IT) departments and other support functions within companies have the most to improve upon as far as their performance in this area. It is easy to ask internal customers what they need and what they expect of their supporting colleagues, yet—as with other KM cases—one of the biggest barriers to knowledge sharing is lack of time. When members of teams like these (those that support organizations) meet, they are usually trying to solve pressing problems quickly. They never have a chance to have a conversation, with their managers or peers or customers, on a deeper level regarding the questions that matter.

The solution to this challenge lies in teaching ourselves and our friends, colleagues, and peers, what quality dialogue is all about. In today's world, the creation of useful intellectual capital through proper knowledge management depends on creating effective conversations. We may use the various interaction methods, presented in Chapter 6, in order to explore how best to communicate effectively. The strong tools we have advocated to use with our external customers, like knowledge cafés and Living Labs, are especially effective for interacting with our internal customers.

Engaging Customers in Defining Strategy

This section is about one of the most significant ways we can use customer knowledge—by involving them in defining the long-term strategy of an organization. We already mentioned in Chapter 3 that instead of limiting the strategy making to top management alone, we had better seek the cumulative knowledge of other stakeholders in the organization—middle managers, leading inside professional and marketing experts, and even all employees if possible. Engaging the customers in creating strategy is an extra step toward an additional, and very important, perspective. It has some risks of exposure, but there are major opportunities to gain such as achieving better trust and bonding.

The Strategy Workshop

Our example is about a large industrial company in Israel, whose business depends mainly on a few large, long-time customers. A newly

(continued)

appointed CEO identified that although these customers usually liked the company's products, there was some tension about the current technical support and possible disagreement about future needs. Hence he coordinated a strategic process in which to collaborate with the largest customers.

They outlined the strategic process in a workshop conducted over two days, with Edna as a facilitator. On the first day, the company invited a group of senior representatives from its customer base. They were seated in a circle, with the company's senior managers sitting in a circle around them. The representatives were asked to imagine themselves, or their successors, in the next following years:

- What could their business and future market look like in that period?
- What would they or their successors need in order to fulfill the needs of that market?
- What is the expected role of the hosting organization in catering to these needs?

To make the most of that workshop, there were predefined rules for the participants. People from the hosting organization, even though they were top managers, were not allowed to intervene in the rounds of discussions (except for clarification questions). Most importantly, they were not allowed to argue or criticize. Most of the time, they just listened.

This questioning and brainstorming continued with a number of the representatives. In the end, the session was fascinating for all of the participants because it was of great benefit for both the organization and its customers to think about the future of the market they were participating in.

The session was recorded, and the next day the company managers met, without the customers, to process what they had learned and to determine how to use the information for their strategic decisions about the future.

This example proves the necessity of special workshops with a customer. Actually, when the idea of such a workshop was first introduced by Edna, the managers at the company resisted it. They claimed that since they were in continuous contact with their customers, there was no added value for coordinating this type of session and they did not think that they had something new to learn. Eventually, however, they were convinced that talking to their customers on a strategic level, rather than a day-to-day level, was a different matter. Moreover, the opportunity of involving multiple perspectives was a clear advantage.

The strict rules of engagement, where the hosting organization managers were supposed to listen without arguing, were also difficult to accept at the beginning. However, this also proved successful by creating an atmosphere of respect that enabled customers to speak freely.

Ultimately, by taking a chance on implementing a method they were not used to, these managers realized that they learned things they had not known. For instance, as the new CEO suspected, one of the issues that came up in the workshop is that the products may be too sophisticated to use. The customers relayed to the company that they were very interested in more training and better technical support for current products, and designing future products for simpler usage.

Conclusion

In this chapter we described various methods for gaining customer knowledge. We believe that one of the factors in the collapse of the technology bubble of the early 2000s may be the fact that many high-tech companies were not communicating with their customers effectively enough. They didn't make sure there was enough of a need for their sophisticated products. The high-tech industry, at that time especially, was technology-driven rather than market-driven. The following is a typical example:

Chromatis—a Broadband too Broad?

At the time of its sale in May 2000, the Israeli start-up Chromatis went to Lucent based on a market value of $4.5 billion.[2] Part of the broadband business, Chromatis provided the service of being able to transmit as much data as possible over the Internet. At the time, everyone agreed this was an important technological development and an important product. It turned out, however, that the speed of data transmission already in use was fast enough. Like many other promising companies at that time, Chromatis closed down about a year later because of lack of customer understanding.

However, listening to customers does not mean that you should limit yourself regarding innovation. Sometimes you can create new needs for your customers without first discussing with them what they need. Obviously, if you only base your developments on customer knowledge acquired through direct communication, then you might be stifling your overall innovation. To this end, organizations should strive to work on two major fronts: making incremental improvements by learning from customers, and also facilitating breakthroughs through the management of innovation. We discuss this last point regarding innovation in more detail in Chapter 10.

The Magnificent 7

1. Your customers are usually willing to share their knowledge with you.
2. Your day-to-day interaction with customers is not enough; you must have scheduled strategic meetings.
3. Invite your customers to knowledge cafés and have them discuss questions that matter.
4. Treat your internal customers as you do your external ones.
5. If possible, run your R&D projects as Living Labs.
6. Allow your customers to become your advisers. Consider creating customer advisory boards within your organization as a solution to lack of communication.
7. Make the process mutually beneficial by sharing your knowledge with your customers so they also know what you need.

CHAPTER 9

Measuring and Managing the Performance of Proper Knowledge Work

In this chapter you will:

Learn about current developments in measuring the effectiveness of knowledge management.

Gain tools for setting goals and objectives and measuring the performance of intangible assets.

Learn methods for measuring the dollar value of intangible assets.

Apply performance assessment to nonprofit units, including departments within organizations.

There is a commonly used business cliché that, unfortunately, is usually right: "If it can't be measured, it can't be managed." We therefore have to define various indicators to measure the knowledge work of an organization and its intellectual capital (IC) creation. However, unlike the customary accounting methods for assessing tangible financial capital, measuring intangible IC is much harder. This chapter describes the challenges and some of the methods to answer them.

The Challenge: Determining What You Need

A manager practicing knowledge management (KM) is looking for a system to measure the work of an organization or team, and assess the results of their efforts to increase their intellectual capital. The manager should expect this assessment system to fulfill two requirements:

- *Management*—to set goals and objectives for managing assets.
- *Assessment of monetary dollar value*—to know the actual influence of these efforts on company value.

These requirements are derived from a manager's experience with traditional accounting methods. These methods were invented at the end of the Middle Ages in Venice and, except for minor adjustments, have not changed much since then. They continue to do a good job of accounting for the tangible aspects of companies, enabling both management and assessment of value.

Unfortunately, although traditional accounting methods work for tangible assets, they are unable to elucidate the true value of the intangible assets of a company in today's information age. Some efforts have been made over the years to overcome this challenge. Accountants are increasingly interested in intangible assets—including research and development, patents, copyright, trademarks, knowledge databases, customer and hardware lists, contracts and agreements, and so on. However, none of the efforts for the accounting of intangible assets has reached the kind of maturity and sophistication that is needed. The increased interest has given us a few processes for deriving an inkling of the true value of a company, but not a coherent, extensive picture.

Assessing Assets

You might recall a few of the advantages and disadvantages of two specific directions of efforts we mentioned previously in Chapter 2: estimating value by reviewing an organization's intellectual capital and creating a system of managing knowledge by using a management tool.

One direction we discussed previously was toward estimating the value of an organization's IC. We discussed the inherent inaccuracy of many of the present methods of estimating IC based on fluctuating market value (MV). Instead, we suggested using Professor Baruch Lev's method to find quantitative dollar results (take the actual annual earnings of a company, deduct the customary yield on physical assets of that industry, and the result is the contribution of the intangible assets).[1] The results helped us establish the business case for proper knowledge management, one that could potentially help investors get a more concrete sense of the intangible assets of a company. But we are still a long way off from seeing this method as an accepted part of company reports. And even if it were accepted, it is not quite timely enough to serve as a basis for future action or for day-to-day business decisions.

The other direction we discussed was toward developing a management tool consisting of a structured set of indicators, representing various focal points of interest for a particular business. These structures, like the Skandia Navigator or Balanced Scorecard, cannot estimate dollar value or derive goals from it. They require that managers make the right strategic decisions, based on their experience and some available data, choosing an appropriate set of indicators to arrive at the proper conclusions. All of these requirements are difficult to determine. Provided managers make the right choices, the management tool might become valuable, enabling managers to set goals and control progress. Nevertheless, they also could fall short of the challenge.

But we hope the disadvantages of some of the methods discussed don't leave readers feeling frustrated.

Frustrating Conclusion? Not Yet!

We admit that there is a reason for frustration. In spite of sophisticated financial reports, it is often difficult to determine the real value of a company in terms of the total sum of its assets (tangible and intangible). Even when used, systems such as the Navigator or Balanced Scorecard just might be too abstract of a tool to come to the correct conclusions.

However, most companies do make reasonable decisions about intangibles insofar as their natural processes are concerned, even when undocumented. Some of them even have practices for managing the natural processes that shed light on the company's worth. Next, we describe some examples upon which we built effective methods for confidence in using the Navigator or Balanced Scorecard systems.

Current Practices: Knowing What You Have

The following sections consist of examples detailing how some companies and organizations have successfully managed their IC assets toward proper KM. In each example we describe the strategic decisions underlying the relevant goals, as well as the way the indicators are chosen and some comments about their relative advantages.

Unlike financial indicators, IC indicators are not always clear-cut. As their name implies, they may be partly intangible. Sometimes the decisions and goals are based on intuition rather than quantitative analysis. Sometimes we cannot measure the desired output, but rather an input we assume might lead to it.

When managing IC, managers should begin with the organization's vision and business strategy. From this general framework a manager would derive the key success factors (KSFs) of the company. These are essentially the business's IC goals.

For each key success factor, a manager would then define several indicators that measure its performance. The indicators are methods of measurement of an organization's current status and its progress regarding the key success factors. The KSFs allow managers to assess to what extent they meet their goals. In this way, they become the units for measuring one's performance in managing intellectual capital.

What follows are examples of the different focal points organizations might assess, in order to more properly measure and control their knowledge work. We present these examples arranged along the Navigator structure, from foundation to top: research and development (R&D), process, customer, human, and financial.

Focusing on R&D to Gain Improvements

Most responsible companies invest in R&D. This is usually a limited resource for which many departments in the organization are competing. The decisions cannot be based on pure analysis but on a mixture of both experience and intuition, as described in the following example:

Example: Making Decisions at DuPont

DuPont's textiles and interiors division has more than $12 billion in annual sales, so it probably spends hundreds of millions of dollars on R&D. We do not know exactly how the managers there decide on investments, but we can assume they have a structured process for allocating such hefty sums.

Professor Baruch Lev's paper, "Sharpening the Intangibles Edge,"[2] described in Chapter 2, gives us some clues as to the questions that R&D managers at a company like DuPont are considering. They include:

- What is the share of a particular manager's division out of the total teams involved in DuPont's R&D?
- How would a manager further divide this share between *product* R&D and *process* R&D?
- How would a manager then allocate resources between various departments inside a given division?

Judging by the success of DuPont's products and services, its managers have probably done a good job in determining where best to allocate their funds. However, they were able to quantitatively show the relative value of some of their investments only after using Professor Lev's calculation methods. Until the calculation methods were available, the managers at DuPont were relying mainly on a mix of intuition and experience in asking these questions and answering them for a desired output.

The moral of this story could be that even large strategic decisions at multimillion-dollar companies are not based solely on pure analysis, but on the tacit knowledge of the top managers and most valuable knowledge workers. However, after those intuitive decisions are made, they are translated into tangible processes that have explicit quantitative goals regarding expenditures and/or milestones that can be managed as a project.

Hence, managers must learn to live with a somewhat ironical process when it comes to trying to manage their intangible assets. Such a process might look like this:

Making a semi-*intangible* decision process,
toward allocating very large *tangible* resources (as toward R&D, as just explained),
intended to aim at achieving an *intangible* IC result,
then managed by a *tangible* project process with decipherable and tracked milestones.

Focusing on Process to Gain Improvements

Many process improvements, like some of the possibilities in the DuPont example above, can be measured in financial terms: Shortening the time to manufacture a product, or lowering the expenses to do it, will have a tangible effect on cost. So a manager can make that strategic decision based on quantitative analysis and measure the improvements accordingly. If the improvement is based on risky R&D, then we again add some intangible elements to the decision.

Some other improvements must be decided upon soft criteria alone. Take Tuvya's experience with peer reviews in Rafael:

Example: Peer Reviews at Rafael

We previously discussed in Chapter 6 how a well-performed peer review is a must toward implementing a good design process. However,

(continued)

this belief is based mostly on our experience of intangibles, with very little quantitative evidence to support it. Because it has an intangible component, we have no firm indicator to measure its results. And since we cannot measure the output (as we said at the beginning of this chapter), there is seemingly no proper way to manage the process.

In a situation where there is little quantitative data, some project managers might claim it is a waste of time to perform various types of reviews. They may only want to retain things like official customer reviews and the like. Conversely, some veteran engineers want to implement additional review processes as a more thorough and longer process in order to come to more well-rounded conclusions.

Even though it is difficult to make the quantitative case for enacting processes like peer reviews, we at Rafael made the strategic decision to do so: in a specified format and at specific stages of particular design processes over the life of a project. Fortunately, our taking a leap of faith based on intuition—and one that did not require huge amounts of time or energy—turned out to be positive for many of the departments at Rafael. In this case we measure the input, making sure that these reviews are conducted on time and methodically, while still looking for an actual indicator with which to measure their effectiveness.

Focusing on Customers to Gain Improvements

When focusing on customers, we have both hard indicators and soft indicators. In a project-oriented organization like Rafael, for example, the value of hard indicators like annual orders and financial logs is carefully budgeted and monitored. The results from these indicators become a part of the company's recorded financial data and represent the success and failure of its past endeavors.

The softer indicators, such as where managers decide to put marketing dollars, the various methods of attracting new customers, and so forth, also represent a company's efforts toward future success but may not have as tangible an outcome.

Focusing on Human Resources to Gain Improvements

At Skandia, we have found many hard indicators that represent soft strategic decisions on human resources. Indicators like the number of employees and their age distribution, compared with the budgeted desired goal, may seem obvious and trivial. Nevertheless, these are objective hard numbers that can point to desired corrective actions, if necessary.

However, any strategic decision determining that desired goal, which may affect the present and future of the organizations, is not trivial. But such strategic decisions cannot be based purely on quantitative data. One organization's goal may be different from another's; goals may even differ from department to department within the same business.

As an example of different approaches toward different desired outcomes, we present a story from Henrik Danckwardt of Skandia AFS, on customizing goals toward remedying employee turnover rates:[3]

Example: Employee Turnover Rate at Skandia AFS

Skandia AFS took measures of its employee turnover rate, but set a different goal for each of its allied companies based on their unique position. Three situations and their pertinent goals are outlined here:

- One AFS company suffered from a high employee turnover rate. Accordingly, its yearly goal was to stabilize the workforce and to reduce the level of turnover.
- Another allied company was plagued by the opposite problem. It wanted a higher turnover rate to attract new and innovative workers to refresh the company. Its goal was toward raising turnover.
- A third company decided that its employee turnover rate was not important for the time being. That year it concentrated on other indicators that were affecting the bottom line of the business.

These situations are all quite different and each has its own unique goal. At a company like Rafael, managers strive for a very low rate of employee turnover. In the Skandia AFS example, each company would get hard numbers as goals, all derived from somewhat soft strategic decisions. Each company's decision process and final setting of goals will have a major influence on the future of its IC.

Focusing on the Bottom Line to Gain Improvements

The focal points we have been discussing are from the Navigator system, which was designed for a commercial company. For such organizations, the *bottom line* is the financial results, represented by traditional financial data like sales, profit, and so on. The strategy and goals here are based on hard numbers familiar to managers. There is no need to elaborate on them except to mention that although finances are at the top of the structure as far as goals are concerned, they represent the outcome of past activities and hence are not sufficient to predict future results.

A more challenging task is to derive indicators for nonprofit organizations where financials are not at the top of the structure in terms of goals. Examples of such organizations include academic institutions, or departments that are cost centers in a for-profit organization.

In general, the question, "What is the bottom line by which an organization's success is measured?" is an important one in raising strategic discussions about the mission of an organization. Take, for example, the following decisions that a department in a university should make:

The Bottom Line for a University Department

Typical strategic questions of a university department are:

- Should it judge itself by the quality of research? Or should it judge itself by the students—their number, quality, and satisfaction?
- Should it strive to be the *best* (in some sense) or the *largest* in some area of expertise or in some community?
- Should it include all these criteria in its assessment? And/or are there other criteria to consider?

Obviously, each decision may lead to different actions, and consequently to a different set of hard or soft indicators to measure their influence on the bottom line. But a bottom line for a university department is usually difficult to measure by hard numbers, especially if you look at the quality of research or quality of teaching. That is why some departments in Israeli universities are conducting a regular inspection of themselves, every several years, by an international committee of renowned professors. The committee is asked to review the various aspects of the department activities, and its observations and recommendation are a substitute for the difficult-to-get hard numbers.

The Navigator: A Framework for IC Management

We've demonstrated important aspects of assessing IC and its management in various focal points. In this section we offer examples of how various organizations comprehensively manage the whole of their IC, in all focal points, using the Navigator.

Before we continue we remind again that while we are accustomed to the Navigator, you may use Balanced Scorecard (BSC) for the same purpose.

We begin with Skandia, which was the pioneer, and continue top-down from a nation to a small department in a large organization. In all cases we emphasize the process from strategy to indicators.

Using the Navigator to Assess the IC of Skandia AFS

Skandia AFS, located in Sweden, was a pioneer in KM in the 1990s when it incorporated the Navigator in its day-to-day management processes throughout the company. These processes are still a good role model, even though Skandia underwent major changes in the mid-2000s. Next, we show you an example of its IC balance sheet and describe the way it used this balance sheet in its management.

SKANDIA AFS'S BALANCE SHEET   Leif Edvinsson, then Skandia VP for intellectual capital, described Skandia's balance sheet to Tuvya in an interview conducted in Skandia headquarters in Stockholm in 1997.[4] (For a visual representation of the balance sheet, please see Figure 9.1. It contains examples of some typical indicators.) The balance sheet complements traditional financial reports by providing managers with new tools for managing IC. Figure 9.1 uses numbers from American Skandia's IC balance sheet for the years 1993 to 1995. This balance sheet was given as a supplement to Skandia's annual report to its shareholders.

We have already gone over the various focal points for a company to consider, so we now comment on some of the most important specifics of the points:

- *Financial focus.* This first focus area incorporates standard financial indicators such as sales and profits. What is striking to us as we review the entire balance sheet is that most companies look only at these parameters in making their managerial decisions.
- *Customer focus.* The "number of contracts" and "number of points of sale" are on the rise in this balance sheet, signifying continuous growth. Based on these indicators we would be optimistic about the flow of revenue over the coming years.
- *Human focus.* You can see some of the data showing different aspects of the employee population by reviewing this section. An interesting observation relates to the information about "training expenses per employee" and the "change in IT literacy." These were high in the first year, reflecting the importance of IT and training for a fledgling financial organization. But they decreased significantly over the years on this balance sheet. Is that a sign of maturity at the company or a telltale indication of neglect in these

Indicator	Year		
Currency in Swedish Kronas, 7 SEK ≈ 1 US$	**1995**	**1994**	**1993**
Financial Focus			
Return on net asset value	20%	12%	24%
Management operating results (MSEK)	247	115	96
Value added per employee (MSEK)	1.63	1.66	1.98
Customer Focus			
Number of contracts (K)	87.8	59.1	32.0
Saving per contract (KSEK)	360	333	371
Number of points of sale (K)	18.0	11.6	4.8
Human Focus			
Number of employees	300	200	133
Number of managers	81	62	NA
Number of managers who are women	28	13	NA
Training expenses per employee (KSEK)	2.5	9.8	10.6
Change in IT literacy	+2%	+7%	NA
Process Focus			
Number of contracts per employee	293	269	241
Administration expenses/gross premium	3.3%	2.9%	2.6%
IT expenses/administration expenses	13%	8.8%	4.7%
Processing time, new contracts [days]	8	6	NA
Processing time, changes [days]	3	13	NA
Renewal and Development Focus			
Premiums from new launches	49%	11%	5%
Increase in net premium	30	18	205
Development expenses/administration expenses [%]	10.1	11.6	9.8
Percentage of staff under 40	79	72	74

FIGURE 9.1 American Skandia Balance Sheet

Source: Adapted from the AFS Balance Sheet (Leif Edvinsson).*

---

*The currency used in this balance sheet is the Swedish Krona. The typical exchange rate at the middle 1990s was approximately 7 Kronas per 1 US$. (Surprisingly, after variation during the years, it is approximately the same rate in 2010).

areas? This was an important question for Skandia's management to assess, and they became aware of it as a direct result of the Navigator's statistics output.

▪ *Process focus*. The data are self-explanatory, but it is instructive to point out that the IC indicators in this section include human capital turned into organizational capital. These are competencies that remain in the organization when employees go home. They include procedures, IT infrastructure and databases, and so on. IT literacy is an indicator for human capital, as mentioned previously, but IT systems are process capital

▪ *Renewal and development focus*. Renewal and development is directly related to the expected future results. In a high-tech company, this focus refers mainly to the R&D function. But the Navigator is framed to be appropriate for all kinds of companies utilizing various levels of technology. As a financial services company, Skandia still identified the importance of and need for innovation within its goals. Most of the indicators are obvious and expected here. An intriguing indicator is "percentage of staff under 40." The fact that this indicator appears here, and not in the human focus, sends a strong message about Skandia's management viewpoint at that time. They considered that continuous vitality of a company required a high percentage of new, and many times younger, people. What is the viewpoint on this issue in your organization?

HOW DOES THE NAVIGATOR WORK?   Henrik Danckwardt, then chief financial officer of Skandia AFS in Sweden, showed Tuvya how they applied the Navigator for managing their IC.[5] Danckwardt's task was to control the status and performance of all the AFS allied companies in 18 countries worldwide. Each local company had considerable freedom to utilize its expertise in the local market, while enjoying Skandia's expertise and technologies.

Danckwardt used several principles in devising his control system:

▪ Although he was chief officer of finance, he broadened his vision to encompass the whole picture, not only the financial parameters. His broad view was based on the structure of the Navigator and enabled both comprehensive and flexible management.
▪ The indicators in the Navigator were customized for the specific need of each local company, while maintaining common managerial goals (e.g., we have mentioned before the customization of "employee turnover rate").
▪ The indicators and goals were not forced from above. They were developed in coordination with the local company.

Every year Skandia headquarters had a discussion with each of the companies, during which they evaluated the previous year's results and

prepared the next year's budgets. These budgets included traditional financial goals as well as all the agreed-upon nonfinancial IC indicators. The
yearly indicators were derived out of this strategy, prepared according to
the IC methodology we described earlier:

Mission and strategy → Key success factors → Indicators → Action

Once the strategy was decided upon, the management tool was incorporated into special software, with the indicators implemented on a web
site. At that time financial data was automatically derived from the preexist-
ing IT system of the corporation, while IC indicators were manually input
by each allied company.

CONCLUSION ON SKANDIA'S EXPERIENCE   According to Danckwardt, most
of the alliances embraced this management system. The key to its favor-
able reception was that it served as a common ground for management.
Each company aimed to achieve the mutually agreed-upon values of its
indicators.

In some of the subsidiaries, such as American Skandia, managers were
actually rewarded according to how well they met the IC goals. Note that
because financial terms constituted only a small part of their expected
bonus, managers were not tempted to sacrifice IC for short-term book
value (BV).

At the time, Skandia seemed like the ultimate realization of knowledge
culture in a company. It had the right combination of vision, culture, and
knowledge management tools. Even though its prosperity somewhat
declined later, its knowledge culture is still worth learning from as a successful example.

Using the Navigator to Assess the IC of a Country

If the concept of intellectual capital and a Navigator to manage it is so
good for a specific company, why not use it for a country? Why not establish formal, systematic measurement criteria to document and report the
progress of a nation according to key success factors that represent the
prosperity of the nation? We describe the experience of two countries that
have tried to do this.

INTELLECTUAL CAPITAL INDICATORS IN SWEDEN   In 1997 a group of students
from the Market Academy of Stockholm University, in collaboration with
Skandia, applied a modified form of the Skandia Navigator at the national
level in order to identify Sweden's critical success factors. The resulting
report was entitled *Welfare and Security*.[6]

The following is a brief summary of their groundbreaking representation of the country's intangible values. Readers can assess for themselves the meaning and relative importance of each indicator.

- The financial focus represents the traditional economic way of measuring a country's wealth, including per capita gross domestic product (GDP), national debt, and the mean value of its currency in terms of the U.S. dollar.
- The customer focus highlights the relationship between Sweden and certain other countries. Success factors included extent of tourism, perceived trustworthiness of businessmen, balance of service, and balance of trade, particularly in terms of intellectual property (patents, royalties, etc.).
- The human focus outlines indicators for assessing the prosperity of the Swedish people. These include quality of life, as defined by some health indicators (average life expectancy, infant survival rate, smoking, etc.), education, crime rate, and resources for the elderly.
- The process focus highlights the efficiency of social structures. These include structural changes in industry toward increasingly knowledge- and service-oriented firms, management practices that foster innovation and quality, widespread use of information technology, road safety, and the employment of women.
- The renewal and development focus assesses Sweden's investment in developing competencies for the future through research and development in industry and science, entrepreneurship, the development of trademarks, and the attitudes of its youth.

The purpose of Sweden's balance sheet is clearly to present the country's tangible and intangible assets in a comprehensive manner and raise awareness of indicators and goals beyond the traditional financial measures. As in business organizations, awareness of these broader intangible assets can guide the successful implementation of strategic decisions.

INTELLECTUAL CAPITAL INDICATORS IN ISRAEL   Israel was the second country in the world, after Sweden, to produce an IC balance sheet. Edna and her consulting team produced the first edition[7] of the balance sheet themselves in 1998, and later editions were sponsored by the Israeli government (with the last one published in 2007).[8]

In order for Israel to maintain its lead position in certain fields, and in order to improve its standing in other fields, it needed to focus on allocating its resources accordingly. The IC report was an important helpful device in identifying the fields that required focus regarding the country's national resources.

Israel's IC focal points are arranged in groups similar to those of the Navigator's (and to the Sweden report we just mentioned). The data is compiled from many sources, including internationally renowned surveys. The following details showcase a few of the innovative indicators that materialized as being on an upswing.

▪ The financial focus, as in the Swedish report, represents the traditional economic indicators of a country's wealth.

▪ The customer focus includes indicators like the number of start-up companies and biotechnology companies, which highlight the extent of the country's participation in a knowledge-based world economy. Note that these same indicators are in some way promising renewal, and may also be included in the renewal and development focus.

▪ For the human focus, the number of female students at institutions of higher education and women in the professional workforce are important indicators, assessing the extent of the country's ability to optimally utilize its human resources through the implementation of equal opportunity as a fundamental value. Additionally, alcohol consumption and youth experimentation with smoking were used as signs of the physical and mental health of the country's population. Events like museum visits were seen as an indicator of the population's consumption of, and interest in participating in, culture.

▪ For the process focus, the extent of Internet use, software use, and the circulation of daily newspapers are indicators of the levels of processes of communications and computerization.

▪ For the renewal and development focus, scientific publications in the world and registration of patents per capita are indicators of the country's ability to contribute to global renewal and development.

These and other indicators are promising avenues for the development and implementation of national policies for future growth, just as they would be for a private organization to ensure future growth of a company.

CONCLUSION ON THE NATIONAL IC EXAMPLES   We look at Israel's IC with mixed thoughts. On the positive side, we are proud that the promises and expectations created by the IC indicators in these reports are proving to materialize. In recent years the Israeli economy has prospered—mostly because of its large investments in IC, both publicly and privately—and was one of the first nations in the Western world to come out of the world financial crisis of 2008.

On the less positive side, we know that these indicators are snapshots of the IC we have now, which is a result of past national policies. Unfortunately, they do not represent our country's current common vision and strategy. We believe this is because Israel is grappling with defining its vision within the context of conflicting internal identities.

Just like organizations, countries should define their strategies for improving their competitive position relative to other countries, to enhance sustainable prosperity of their citizens. Without such a strategy, the IC balance sheet loses its significance as a potential source for policy.

Using the Navigator to Visualize and Increase IC of an Old Industry Corporation

In Chapter 1 we have presented the strategic problem that faced Danya Cebus in the late 1990. Danya Cebus is a leading Israeli construction company that has implemented many large, complex projects including malls, government offices and ministries, and industrial science parks. When it decided to go public, it sought a method for raising its apparent value to potential investors, who at the time were more attracted to the booming high-tech industries.

It decided to create an IC balance sheet as an elegant way of presenting itself and its potential for growth. IC balance allowed Danya Cebus to visualize its core competencies, which were its hidden values. It showed, essentially, that Danya Cebus was a high-tech company in the low-tech construction industry. It revealed that it was a company on the rise in a declining market. As expected, the IC balance sheet significantly raised the value of the company and led to satisfactory results on the stock market.

The following are some sample indicators, demonstrating core competencies that are not shown on the traditional financial report:

- *Human:*

  Worker loyalty as expressed by the average period of work at the organization (for managers: 20 years!);
  The number of engineers employed;
  The number of workers with graduate degrees;
  Managerial training (at least one training day a month).

- *Process:*

  Use of advanced technology and information systems;
  Lesson-learning procedures;
  Quality management systems.

- *Customer and Suppliers:*

  Joint collaborations with foreign companies;
  Subcontractor loyalty.

Although Danya Cebus's IC Balance Sheet began as a creative marketing tool aimed at raising its market value, it eventually came to be used as a management tool. The company's managers found that they can use the indicator to delineate goals and work plans for strengthening the company's core competencies.

Using the Navigator to Assess the IC of a Nonprofit Unit at Rafael

The IC management of a department within an organization is intertwined with the organization's overall business strategy. Nonetheless, departments can delineate their own vision, strategy, and IC indicators within the larger policy to reflect their unique character and needs.

The strategies of divisions of large organizations, which are managed as independent business units, are essentially scaled-down versions of the IC management strategy of the organization as a whole.

This is not the case with units for which performance is not assessed according to their profits. These units may be engineering R&D departments in a matrix organization, human resources departments, and so forth. They, too, can (and should) use Navigator-like tools to set goals and measure their performance. However, they must define their strategy and their bottom-line results.

While we do not claim to have a structured and comprehensive answer to this issue, we can present some lessons learned at Rafael. We give the following examples of creating IC indicators in a large R&D center versus creating the indicators in a typical smaller section of that center.

On the one hand, we have a large R&D center at one division of Rafael, consisting of more than 1,000 scientists and engineers of various disciplines. All of them are doing research, development, and engineering work for internal customers, who are all actual business units of that division. On the other hand we have a section, which is a small unit with 25 to 50 workers, usually dedicated to a specific discipline. (We also have a middle hierarchical level between them, which we shall not discuss here.)

STRATEGY   Defining the strategy and vision, as a prerequisite for defining indicators, was easier for the center than for its sections. The R&D center strategy and vision are derived somewhat from the division strategy with some center's unique additions. While it was not fully codified, it was clear enough for the center's top managers. They were also experienced enough to define the necessary updates over the years.

Defining section's strategy was more difficult. Some section managers, while doing well in their day-to-day operations, had a difficult time with the more abstract task of creating an actual strategy and vision. Still others had difficulty deriving the key success factors toward creating IC indicators.

Further, contrary to what you might think, in some cases veteran technicians managing a support department did better with this task than some of the younger PhD employees managing groups of scientists. A more serious analysis of the problems taught us two lessons:

1. Many of the difficulties resulted from creating this process from the bottom up, instead of waiting for a defined center strategy and then going top-down.
2. Strategy is really a difficult task for inexperienced managers who require better training and mentoring.

BOTTOM-LINE INDICATORS   Bottom-line indicators for these nonprofit units, replacing the financial indicators of business units, were simpler to get for the small section than for the large center as a whole. The small section usually has well-defined tasks, by which it is judged by internal customers (completing a design and being ready for a formal review, building a subassembly and testing it as a unit, etc.).

The indicators presented here for the bottom line of the large center are more complex, and evolved from years prior. First, the division required this major large center to measure itself according to the overall division's financial results—sales, profit, and so on. Even though the R&D center is not the only one influencing the division's financial results, and many times it has no direct influence, it must be aligned with them. This assures it will do its best to add to the success of the division.

Second, the large center managers decided they needed some indicators with a more direct relationship between center activities and internal customers—the division and its project managers. They came up with two, one measuring input and the other, output:

1. Input: the success in meeting individual project demands for R&D personnel. This indicator is checked frequently, almost daily, by the center and its customers and the results lead to corrective actions.
2. Output (obvious for an aerospace organization): performing flight tests on time and with successful results.

INDICATORS FOR THE OTHER NAVIGATOR FOCUS AREAS   Some of the bottom-line indicators described thus far also serve to achieve customer goals. In a perfect process, we would also hope to factor formal internal customer satisfaction surveys into these indicators. But at the time of this exercise, we had failed to employ it as timely tool. However, please do keep it in mind for your organization when doing a similar exercise.

To the preceding bottom-line indicators, we would brainstorm on all other focus areas regarding planning work processes, human resources, and R&D. These tasks were simpler than the previous ones, for both the center level and the section level. In many cases, the section level indicators could have been directly derived from the center indicators. Further, many indicators are similar to those already mentioned for other organizations. Examples include the following:

- Renewal and development: Unlike the abstract strategy, no manager (junior or senior) in an R&D center has difficulties setting ambitious short-term and long-term research goals and deriving indicators to measure them.
- Human resources: In addition to the usual indicators like depicting number and professions of new recruits, we follow the processes of screening and training top employees for future leadership assignments.
- Work processes: In some departments that seem to grow too fast, we set goals for outsourcing some of the work.

A Final Note on the Navigator as a Universal Framework

The preceding discussions prove the effectiveness of the Navigator as a universal framework to manage the IC of various and different organizations, be it a country, a company, or a department within a company.

For example, sections, centers, and divisions at Rafael are vastly different from those at Skandia and its subsidiaries (for which the Navigator was originally developed). The two companies engage in completely different work (in this case, financial services versus the aerospace industry), they are different sizes, and they are located in geographically distinct areas and within divergent cultural contexts. In spite of these differences, though, the Navigator proved to be a useful framework for measuring and setting performance goals for both of their intangible assets. Rafael's only modification while using the Navigator framework, in light of its unique characteristics, was adding an additional focal point: technology and infrastructure.

This type of nimble adjustment, depending on the core competencies of a company, can only make the Navigator framework even more valuable.

Conclusion

Unfortunately, in terms of assessing the *monetary dollar value* of intangible assets, these methods of assessing IC indicators are not fixed and polished accounting tools, but this is to be expected when you are using innovative methods and treading new ground. Even though the systems are not up to speed with all the needs, managers and investors must become familiar with such tools while waiting for improvements in these accounting systems.

In terms of *managing intangible assets*, though, we have attempted to demonstrate to managers the various methods currently available to them in order to start them on their path toward proper knowledge management. Using structured frameworks like the Navigator or the Balanced Scorecard can help managers learn from what their organizations are already doing. The principle behind these frameworks is the same no matter the method: They assist managers in defining their strategy regarding intangible assets and IC, by helping them set goals to derive appropriate indicators to measure and manage their goals.

The methods presented in this chapter for managing intellectual capital may be adapted to different types of organizations—from local to global and public to private, as well as both profit and nonprofit.

This chapter concludes the third phase of our knowledge management journey, where we have presented several chapters describing the various view points of knowledge. The next chapter, on Innovation, is the last phase and final peak of the journey.

The Magnificent 7

1. Managing intellectual capital requires an appropriate system for measuring intangible assets.
2. Responsible organizations already have some methods of measuring and managing their intangible assets, or at least part of them. Managers should identify the existing method, and use them as a basis for a more comprehensive and/or more structured method.
3. Skandia's Navigator is a comprehensive and convenient method for measuring intellectual capital and setting goals that can be utilized by a variety of organizations.
4. The Navigator involves a sequential process of deriving critical success factors based on an organization's vision and strategy and devises indicators to assess performance and set goals according to these factors.
5. The Navigator framework divides intangible assets into five focus areas: financial, process, human, customer, and renewal and development.
6. New accounting methods are being developed for assessing the monetary value of intangible assets and improving predictions of an organization's success.
7. Nonfinancial units also need a method to assess the performance of their knowledge management endeavors, and may adapt the Navigator to do it.

CHAPTER 10

Innovating for a New Beginning

In this chapter you will:

Learn that constant innovation is a must for the survival of an organization. Organizations and managers cannot afford to neglect investing in innovation, even during difficult periods.

Understand that innovation consists of three components: reuse of existing knowledge, invention of new knowledge, and exploitation of overall knowledge.

Realize that innovation is not limited to technology but can and should happen in all business activities, including business development, human resources, customer relations, marketing, and work processes.

Learn how to establish a culture of innovation that encourages and enables workers to innovate.

This chapter reviews the concept of innovation as a core aspect of knowledge organizations. Learning how to foster and manage innovation is one of the most important tasks of a manager in a knowledge organization, and lies at the heart of proper knowledge management. The chapter reviews methods for requiring, enabling, and encouraging innovation in your organization.

Innovation as the Essence of Knowledge Organizations

Successful knowledge organizations require a culture of continuous renewal, whether of products, technology, or methods. They need some kind of innovation in order to survive and should check their progress periodically according to whether they are meeting this goal.

In this section, we present some examples of role models known for their culture of continuous innovation. These role models, together with the IBM example described in Chapter 3, are aimed to convince you that innovation is the essence of knowledge organizations. We will see that the innovation in these examples, while manifested mainly in their products, lies not only in technology and R&D but in all focus areas of intellectual capital (IC).

Apple Inc.

Apple Inc. has been an example of innovation for more than 30 years since its establishment in 1977. Currently Apple is one of the largest technology corporations in the world, with more than 30,000 employees and more than $40 billion in annual sales. It has redefined its products and markets many times and in many ways, and will continue to do so.

Apple pioneered the personal computer industry with its computers in the late 1970s and revolutionized it with the Macintosh in the 1980s, the PowerBook in the early 1990s, and the iMac in the late 1990s. All the revolutions were comprehensive and successful, in performance, design, and user-friendly interface.

In the 2000s Apple entered into the sphere of consumer electronics and reinvented the market with the iPod and the iPhone; at the time of this writing, it had also just introduced the iPad. All three have been highly influential both in personal computing and in the general consumer electronics industry. A known innovator in marketing, Apple continually outdoes itself with unique advertising campaigns and special concept stores worldwide.

Intel Corporation

Intel Corporation is the world leader in semiconductors, especially microprocessors, with more than 80,000 employees worldwide and more than $35 billion in sales.[1] Founded by Gordon Moore and Robert Noyce in 1968, the company's major breakthrough began with the dawn of the personal computing era in early 1980s.

Intel's culture of continuous innovation is inspired by Moore's Law:

Moore's Law

This law was presented in a 1965 paper by Intel co-founder Gordon Moore. It is not really a physical law, dictated by nature, but a prediction of trend: The law predicts that the number of transistors on a chip board will double every two years, thus promising exponential growth in performance and/or an exponential decrease in size.

> Moore based his prediction on the evaluation of products from 10 years before 1965, and presented the conclusion that he expected it to hold for the next 10 years. His prediction is still valid now—more than 40 years later—because Intel has made Moore's Law somewhat of a self-fulfilling prediction!

Moore's Law inspired developers at Intel so much, that they have been guiding their efforts by setting an ever-increasing and ever-demanding goal to achieve. Their dedication to continuous innovation in chip design and manufacturing processes have been fulfilling Moore's Law ever since.

Rafael

Rafael is now a successful, profitable aerospace company, with sales over $1.6 billion in Israel and worldwide.[2] It is a rather small company compared to world aerospace giants. Nevertheless, it has been successful over decades in developing and marketing leading products, many of which are the first and/or the best in the world in their category.

Rafael's competitive edge is built mainly on innovations in technology and system engineering. These are the fruits of knowledge management and intellectual capital built over time. In addition to technology and R&D, Rafael has innovated in many other ways. It has reinvented itself several times over the years. The last transformation occurred in 2001, when it went from being a state-subsidized R&D unit to a profitable business returning annual dividends to its shareholder (the Israeli Treasury). The process and its success have been described in Chapter 3, and culminated in 2009 with record sales, profits, a backlog of orders, and independent R&D budget.

Such transformation requires innovations in the financial governance, marketing, and work processes of a company. Combined with continuing excellence in R&D, these types of innovations at Rafael have enabled it to deploy new products in record time, among other things.

Israel

Israel as a nation has become a role model of innovation, as described in the book by Senor and Singer, *Start-Up Nation*.[3] They analyze how innovations in R&D, business entrepreneurship, and other fields made a great impact on what seems impossible: A small country, with no natural resources and in a continuous state of war, has more start-ups than giants like Canada, China, and the United Kingdom!

Knowledge Management as an Innovation Enabler

In today's knowledge economy, if you don't innovate, you die. The strategic race is about finding and utilizing unorthodox ideas that create the future by changing the rules of an industry; it's about redrawing boundaries between industries, and creating entirely new industries. To understand the future and create it, companies must unlearn some of their current modes of thought and develop foresight into tomorrow's markets. Companies need to focus their innovation efforts toward creating new ideas, enabling experiments to test these ideas, and implementing the promising ideas as ventures. Top management's mission therefore becomes about creating organizational structures and processes that are capable of spawning innovation.

Defining Innovation

Innovation is the opposite of conservatism (or what we refer to as more-of-the-same). Formally, it can be defined as beginning with reuse or new use of existing knowledge, adding an invention, and then creating a new product or service that exploits this invention. These three components for innovation are all connected. If one of them is not present, innovation cannot happen. The three components of innovation, further defined, can be characterized as follows:

1. Reuse and new use of knowledge is about using your competencies in new ways or in order to invent new things. It is about using them to make money by creating products or services that people want and need.
2. Invention requires creativity.
3. Exploitation is essential if you are in a profit-driven environment looking to grow your business, employee base, and shareholder revenues.

The Second Generation of Knowledge Management Is Innovation

We have already discussed the first generation of knowledge management in previous chapters: capturing, storing, and reusing existing knowledge. Projects of pioneering organizations included systems of managing knowledge like company yellow pages, experts outlining processes they are involved in, creating learning communities where employees/customers share their knowledge, creating information systems for documenting and storing knowledge, and so on. These first-generation KM initiatives were about viewing knowledge as the foremost strategic asset, measuring it, capturing it, storing it, and protecting it. They were about treating knowledge as an asset, recognizing how it influences strategy, and wanting to make the most of it by managing it properly.

The second generation of knowledge management shifts from managing knowledge to creating new knowledge: innovation. Behind innovation lies the awareness that old knowledge becomes obsolete. Innovation focuses on shortening lead times, accelerating new product development, and creating new organizational structures that save money.

The next section demonstrates how innovation is fostered with proper knowledge management and intellectual capital.

Focal Points of Innovation

Innovation has many facets, and a knowledge organization must excel in at least one of them to survive. The most obvious of them is the introduction of new products and services, usually associated with research and development (R&D) efforts. However, as we've said before, innovation is manifested not only in R&D, but may involve every activity of the organization—processes, human resources, and so on. We can again use the Navigator framework to classify the various focus areas of innovation.

The following discussion demonstrates how organizations are innovating in the various focal points and how some organizations are excelling in more than one.

Innovation and R&D

Product innovation based on R&D is the most visible facet of innovation. All role models in this area exhibit substantial investments in R&D to achieve major product success.

3M is a very different business from the other role models we've mentioned, yet it is still a veteran example of an innovative knowledge company. It is constantly ensuring innovation by requiring that 30 percent of its sales every year come from new products. The company sets a quantitative measurement for the achievement of future innovation and, as we shall see, invests heavily in R&D to achieve it.

Investing in R&D in order to foster innovation may seem obvious, but the real test of a company's commitment to constant innovation comes during difficult times. The story of Applied Materials during the aftermath of the high-tech bubble in the early 2000s demonstrates the difficult innovation decisions a knowledge company faces in hard times:

Example: Applied Materials—The Importance of Maintaining R&D Even During Recession

Applied Materials (AMAT) is the largest supplier of products and services to the global semiconductor industry and is one of the world's leading information infrastructure providers. Its Israeli technology center was established in 1991. The center's mission is to develop control systems integrating hardware and software for the company's automated systems. The core staff includes highly experienced, professional engineers committed to market-driven innovation.

During the early 2000s, like the rest of the high-technology world, Applied Materials had to face the economic slowdown. The following is what we wrote at the end of 2001 about the situation:[4]

> *Dan Vilenski, then the chairman of AMAT Israel, has been proud of AMAT's success. He has credited AMAT's careful preparation during economic upturns, its continuous investment in R&D and innovation, and its commitment to its workers. When the company was financially solid, investments in R&D as a percent of sales continued to grow. And during the 1999 crisis, AMAT invested in 300-mm technology, which directly raised 2000 sales from $6 billion to $10 billion.*

> *But the continuation of the economic crisis has put AMAT's commitment to R&D and its workers to a test. AMAT began by cutting significantly in its costs and expenses, initiating plant shutdowns, employee-wide pay cuts, and raising the effectiveness of inventory management. What it did not do, however, was cut its R&D expenses or lay off workers.*

> *"We did not—nor will we—cut R&D," was Vilenski's approach. "It is important to continue to develop new products that will fuel the business when we get out of the recession." As part of this strategy, AMAT acquired Oramir, a small Israeli company whose technology complemented AMAT and was anticipated to generate additional business during any future upturn. They planned to use the recession time to integrate the culture of the two companies. And they knew that they must continue to invest in their workers, knowing they wouldn't get far without investing in the abilities of their people.*

> *But as 2001 came to a close and the recession continued to worsen, AMAT's strategy proved difficult to maintain. As survival consider-*

> *ations became paramount and rose to the forefront, AMAT must*
> *have asked itself: Will we be able to continue investing in the future?*
> *Is R&D a luxury we can no longer afford?*
>
> Looking back a decade later we see that AMAT Israel, even though
> it continued R&D investments,[5] was forced to make some small-scale
> layoffs in late 2002.[6] However, looking at global AMAT sales, we see
> that although they fell from the aforementioned 2000 value of $10
> billion to about $5 billion, they rose again to the $8 billion to $10 billion
> level in 2004 and later.[7] Part of the recovery is obviously due to the
> company's continuous R&D innovation.

What we see here is a real-life situation with difficult decisions. On
one hand, Applied Materials acknowledged in its declared strategy for
managing during the economic crisis that continuous innovation is a must
for its survival in the long run. In the knowledge market in which AMAT
operates, cutting costs should never be at the expense of competency R&D,
and that includes continual investment in the knowledge workers who
constitute it. On the other hand, it may be necessary (or at least tempting)
in such hard times to view R&D and employee development as luxuries.
It seems that Applied Materials generally acted according to its declared
strategy: While probably doing some cutbacks, it continued investing in
R&D with good results later.

Innovation and Process

There are many facets of process innovation. The following examples
demonstrate two very different facets.

EXAMPLE: ELBIT—INNOVATION USING CONTINUOUS ORGANIZATIONAL CHANGES
Some companies keep themselves alert and innovative by making continuous organizational changes. This is their way of adapting to the changes
in the outside business environment and to the internal structures of their
departments, managers, and workers. Elbit of Israel is a distinguished
example:

Elbit Organizational Changes

Elbit, a successful privately owned Israeli defense corporation (with a
$2.5 billion market value in 2010), has made the process of continuous

(continued)

organizational changes a core competence of its innovation approach. Here, they are described by Yossi Ackerman, current Elbit CEO, in a newspaper interview in 2010:[8]

> *He claimed that his managers do not hang paintings in their offices because they know they will not be staying there for a long enough time. The feeling was that managers changed positions and offices so quickly, and history had proved that such changes were good for the welfare of the company and its people alike.*
>
> *He discussed how Elbit was making frequent organizational changes, about twice a year, in order to adapt to two important things: the market and people. His theory was that Elbit should not adapt the people to the organization but the organization to the people.*
>
> *Contrary to other organizations, Elbit was making organizational changes relatively easily because it was a well-known fact of the positions there. When making a change, they would keep employees informed along the way so as to lower the fear factor; many of the employees saw the possibility of the change as an opportunity instead of a risk.*

But anyone involved in a major organizational change also knows the price of such an open attitude to change in an organizational structure. It arises at the employee level as debate, excitement/fear, and rumor mills. So we don't encourage it as an overall innovation focal point for an organization.

However, for the same reason, we must appreciate Elbit's capability to make reorganizations so frequently and so effectively, without suffering from the negative effects that are usually associated with it. It is one of their unique core competencies for innovation, and Elbit's continuous success for many years proves it works for them.

EXAMPLE: WAL-MART'S SUPPLY CHAIN   Wal-Mart, the largest corporation in the United States and the world's largest retailer, owes a major part of its success to innovation in processes. Its most major innovations are in terms of giving its shoppers the lowest prices—lower than they could get anywhere else.

In order to do this, it uses the most sophisticated available technology to make its supply chain, including inventory tracking and distribution system, the most efficient and most effective. Several examples of these innovations involve:

- Pioneering the use of the universal bar code, and fully capturing and exploiting all the information behind it.
- Introducing the use of radio frequency identification technology (RFID), which enables tags on products or pallets to hold and transmit much more data than bar codes.
- Employing a private satellite network, beginning in the 1980s, connecting all its operating units with its headquarters.

Innovation and Customers

Customer innovation is a known subject: It is the essence of most marketing efforts for businesses, and marketing is included in the curricula of business courses taught in universities worldwide. Hence there is no need to elaborate on this subject here, and the following list offers just a few examples to demonstrate it. Innovations in terms of customers use existing knowledge, usually technological, for new purposes appealing to different or additional customers:

1. *Appealing to different customers.* Hewlett-Packard Development Company (HP) established itself in the 1950s and 1960s as a leader in specialized, high-end scientific instruments. It entered the much larger market of offices and homes when it invented handheld calculators in the early 1970s, and later developed as a full provider in the market of printers.
2. *Enlarging an existing customer base.* Spreading from your home country market to markets abroad is a centuries-old practice. Because of this, one may ask, why is it that going global should be considered an innovation? However, actually making it happen is not a trivial matter, and requires lots of customer knowledge and innovation to be successful. It is sufficient to mention the different results of several popular American food chains that tried to penetrate the Israeli market during the 2000s: McDonald's knew how to adapt (i.e., new use) its products to the local tastes and prospered, while Starbucks and Dunkin' Donuts failed to adjust and ended up failing miserably overall.
3. *Entirely new services.* Dell and Amazon are customer-driven companies. Dell pioneered the service of producing personal computers on demand, to exact customer specifications. Amazon reinvented the concept of convenient online purchases, beginning with books and expanding into almost everything else.

Methods for Enabling Innovation

Because the business environment in which organizations operate is dynamic, the most important threat organizations face is getting comfortable because of past successes. Paradoxically, success can be a dangerous thing. To paraphrase Andy Grove, Intel's former CEO, you need to be paranoid in order to survive, and success makes it hard to be paranoid. Success leads to complacency and self-congratulation. Renewal means that the organization houses individuals who wake up every morning with the questions, "What will I renew today?" and "What did I renew yesterday?"

But companies cannot expect innovation to happen by itself. To renew constantly, you have to adopt innovation as a core value, and you need methods to do so. Consequently, this section is about requiring innovation in the organization and how to foster it.

Making Innovation a Requirement

The following examples demonstrate various ways of encouraging continuous innovation by making it a required activity. The first example demonstrates this basic requirement:

Example: GE—Innovation as Part of the Job

In light of the importance of innovation in knowledge companies, it makes sense that successful companies treat it as an obligation rather than an option. When Tuvya visited the General Electric subsidiary in Haifa, which develops medical equipment, he found out that GE's headquarters requires the Haifa office to demonstrate a major improvement every year. Every year they must show that they either have developed a new product or made a major improvement on an existing one.

Note that this is a smart requirement. Something new is not sufficient; innovation must have enough value to be incorporated in a product.

In some of Rafael's departments we tried to include the requirement for innovation in the formal periodic review process, with some interesting results:

Example: Rafael—Innovation as Part of the Periodic Review Process

Rafael's divisions, probably like most organizations, conduct formal quarterly or semiannual reviews of their departments' activities. The late Gadi Barak, whom we have already mentioned as a division manager, decided to focus on long-term issues in these reviews (the intellectual capital) and especially innovation. He placed less emphasis on the current operational problems, because they were discussed more frequently in different forums.

He required each department to show two or three new developments during that period. The innovations could be technological or involve work processes, but what was most important was that they were not "more of the same." At that time this type of focus on innovation was not always understood by colleagues, so the implementation was only partially successful. However, it sent the important message that success is about creating something new.

Several years later Tuvya tried to incorporate similar requirements in semiannual reviews of the departments in his R&D center. This time it seemed that there was no problem implementing the idea: Most department managers and even junior section managers liked it, and were proud to present some innovations in technology or processes. However, some of them were too enthusiastic and came up with many activities that might be new but whose real value was not clear.

Adapting GE requirement into our environment, department managers have agreed that each innovation should be accompanied by some estimate of its value: Either a hard indicator, measuring its contribution in terms of dollars, possible saving in labor resources, or shortening time to market; or a soft indicator, where relevant experts may testify it creates a major improvement in quality or performance of products. After a year, we were glad to see that the innovations accumulated to something significant.

The lessons from these two examples are obvious: demand innovation and make sure it is valuable!

Fostering Strategic Discussions on Innovation

Innovation in organizations is usually not one man's show but a team effort. In Chapter 6 we discussed the social model of communities of practice

(CoPs) as a basis for creating and sharing knowledge in groups. This model claims that learning, innovation, and collaboration are social processes that occur in the formal and informal networks of people—the CoPs. The insights from that chapter apply here as well: enabling innovation is about enabling the interactions between knowledge workers that have the potential to generate new knowledge and new directions.

In this section we present some methods of organizing productive strategic discussions on innovation.

INNOVATION REQUIRES FREQUENT DISCUSSIONS   How does an organization create innovation from within? In her consulting experiences, Edna realized companies have rapidly increased the rate of their strategic discussions through the years. In 1978, for example, a company's strategic planning happened every five years. It used to be a major effort, but eventually many organizations developed five-year strategic programs only to find themselves in the same place five years later—which can be frustrating.

Consequently, a few years later, the frequency went down to three, and so on. Now, once every few months, companies are asking themselves how they can renew more quickly. Actually, many companies retain the five-year strategic program, but update it annually for the next five-year period.

INNOVATION REQUIRES MULTIPLE PERSPECTIVES   Although it sounds counter-intuitive, innovation can be managed. This means creating an environment that does not suffocate but encourages innovation. Managing innovation involves establishing and formalizing multiple perspectives.

One challenge of discussions among established teams is that they all know each other well and can predict what one another will say. This predictability makes innovation difficult to create. Sometimes outsiders can help a group break out of its mold. An *outsider* may be outside the organization, like a customer or a consultant. An outsider may also come from another part of an organization, or from a different age group or a different seniority, as described in the following examples.

Skandia Three-Generation Concept

In the 1990s, Skandia utilized a three-generation (3G) concept, introduced by Leif Edvinsson.[9] Their quarterly strategic planning sessions included three generations of workers: recent college graduates, older veterans, and middle-level managers who were connected to an ongoing operation of the company.

The Israeli Military

The same 3G concept is sometimes applied in the Israeli military. Edna describes one particular discussion session as follows:

A commanding general of a large military unit brought three young officers into an important strategic discussion about R&D in the military. They were lieutenants of the lowest levels: one college graduate, one with a little experience, and one with slightly more experience. Some of the more arrogant senior officers were dismayed to see the three inexperienced lieutenants brought into the discussion. However, the facilitator made sure that each question was first addressed to the young lieutenants. By having the senior officers listen to the younger perspectives, the discussion ended up raising interesting ideas about the research process, how it is done, and how it could change.

Overall, gaining multiple perspectives includes mixing the discussion groups so that people of different ages, backgrounds, and experience bring value to the discussion, thereby creating greater opportunity for innovation.

EXAMPLE: R&D CENTER ANNUAL WORKSHOP In his R&D center at Rafael, Tuvya tries to practice what he preaches so he conducts annual strategic discussions according to the rules previously mentioned. Their main features are:

R&D Center Annual Workshops—Main Features

The Goal: Strategic Changes

The workshops are aimed at strategic innovative changes, not just incremental gains. The main theme is usually different each year, dedicated to the main challenge at the time: "Managing human resources" at a time with major outside competition on workforce; "Doing more with the same people" when the company expected major growth and wanted to do it without major recruitments; or "Being better professionals" after some technical failures. The concept of a theme is important, because we want to concentrate on a specific subject that should affect our work for at least the entire next year.

(continued)

The Participants Represent Multiple Perspectives:

Even though the core participants are the top management of the R&D center (about 14 people), we always have guests—seniors, who are usually our internal customers (project managers, corporate managers, and outside experts or facilitators) and/or juniors (middle managers of the center). The guests present their views on the theme, and some of them stay as full-time participants. Tuvya admits that even in those cases where he initially doubted their contribution, he always found later that their perspective was constructive and innovative.

Valuable Results:

The workshops really ended in some innovative suggestions, that led to "not more of the same" action items with valuable results. For example, we discovered that most of the methods for "doing more with the same people" are not just about working harder, but about using the same technological breakthroughs that coincide with "being better professionals." Incorporating these methods both increased quality and saved recruiting about 100 people.

Tangible Encouragement of Individual Innovation

Many organizations have methods to encourage individuals to innovate. We describe some examples, with their advantages and pitfalls, next. The first example is simple, used in Rafael and some variations of it probably exist in other organizations:

Innovation Prizes at Rafael

Rafael's methods of encouraging innovation include innovation prizes, with various levels, giving public recognition (and sometimes monetary sums) for innovative achievements. They are usually given for brilliant new ideas in technology or systems.

These prizes definitely send the message that innovation is encouraged, and they do make the recipients and the organization proud. Nevertheless, there are sometimes second thoughts. Some suggest also emphasizing successful reuse, thus preventing unnecessary invention. Others suggest encouraging recognizing innovation in processes and not just in technology.

The second example is more sophisticated, taken from 3M which is a classic role model for enabling innovation. Some of its measures are described in detail in Collins and Porras's book *Built to Last.*[10] We mention just one of the more famous measures here:

3M Granting Time for Innovation

The company grants each of its knowledge workers 15 percent of their time for R&D ideas. That means that they can spend 15 percent of their time on whatever they want. The idea is that if everybody does this—work on whatever interests them—it will help the accumulation of new ideas, some of which become practical products.

This enabling method supports 3M's requirement that 30 percent of its sales will be generated from new products. The 15 percent practice encourages every knowledge worker to incorporate his own knowledge into creating value for the company.

There is an important disclaimer to make. At the risk of jeopardizing the clout of our most cherished message—that knowledge organizations should and must foster innovation—we must qualify that by stating that every organization should consider what is appropriate for its character and needs. For example, 3M's idea is great—for 3M. It might also be great for another company in which development time is short and all you need is a good idea, like 3M's Post-Its.

In other organizations, however, the 15 percent idea may not be appropriate. For instance, Rafael cannot use it since new products require the interdisciplinary knowledge of many people. Some methods were suggested at Rafael to resolve what is called "formalizing the chaos": encouraging the ideas with the best prospects out of the myriad ones that are suggested. We must admit that in retrospect the successful ones were championed by *intra-preneurs*, who had a good idea and combined it with knowledge, while convincing top management and assembling small teams to begin the work. However, it is Rafael's generally open culture—broadly based on technical excellence and innovation—that contributed most to its large number of innovations.

Conclusion

In this chapter, we shared with you our deep belief that the most challenging of all knowledge work is creating new knowledge that adds value (simply put, going from knowledge management to innovation management).

This chapter on innovation is the last phase, and the peak, of our KM journey. However, as we have mentioned in the preface, it is a spiral road so the end just leads to a beginning.

The next chapter concludes the book by describing a road map to start you on your own KM journey, and hopefully take you through it safely.

The Magnificent 7

1. In a dynamic environment, organizations should be continuously innovating.
2. Innovation is not the exclusive territory of R&D departments. It can happen in any business activity of an organization.
3. Innovation has three components: reusing or newly using existing knowledge, creativity or invention, and exploitation to create value for customers. A balance between these elements ensures that existing knowledge is not wasted, that the organization renews, and that innovation has a business rationale.
4. Continuous innovation on the organizational level means frequent strategic discussions in which both content and processes are examined.
5. The manager should foster a culture that requires innovation.
6. The manager should instill various mechanisms that encourage and enable workers to innovate. These mechanisms are based on interactions and multiple perspectives.
7. Investment in innovation should be continuous, even during economically difficult periods.

CONCLUSION

Implementing Knowledge Management—A Step-by-Step Process

In this book you have gained a basic understanding of knowledge management (KM) and intellectual capital (IC). You have read the prerequisites and have gained an appreciation for the strategic and cultural facets of the topic. You have read about the focal points that are most relevant to your organization, and have delved into the issues that interest you most. Finally, you have learned about innovation as the final and paramount task of a knowledge-managing manager.

Now you are ready to embark on your own journey in knowledge management. But how do you begin to practice what you have learned? This Conclusion is aimed at guiding you in the first steps toward implementation.

The Basic Principles

First, no matter how you choose to begin your journey, you must always remember to practice knowledge management (1) from a strategic point of view, (2) utilizing principles of intellectual capital, and (3) with an emphasis on innovation. Beyond these three preconditions, you should attempt those knowledge management practices that you think will be most beneficial to your organization.

Second, remember that you, the manager, must be the leader of knowledge management in your organization or unit. Even if you are a senior manager of a large organization and intend to hire a chief knowledge officer, you should still take on a leadership role. If you are a manager of a middle-size or small organization, or if you are the manager of a unit within an organization, then you should practice knowledge management yourself.

Finally, no matter who does the actual knowledge managing, KM should become an integrated and inherent part of the culture, work processes, and information technology of your organization. Just as any successful knowledge organization engages in human resources (HR) management and in research and development (R&D) management, so it should engage in knowledge management. Recognizing the primacy of intellectual capital requires that the management of this asset become an inherent part of the way the organization functions.

The remainder of this chapter provides a few guidelines for beginning your implementation of knowledge management.

How to Do It

As we highlighted in Chapter 3, knowledge management should begin with an understanding of an organization's strategy and vision and how knowledge management can contribute to their attainment. Choosing exactly where and how to begin is a crucial decision, and it should stem from a vision of the business as an intelligent organization. Ask yourself, "What does an intelligent organization look like?" Once you have this vision, begin drafting your work plan.

The Vision

If you do not work with a vision, attempts to manage knowledge are doomed to fail. These failures are disappointing and lead to disillusionment with the topic being considered. If the knowledge management interventions do not derive from an articulated vision, as well as an understanding of the contribution of KM to the bottom line, they are not worth the time and effort they consume. Clearly knowledge management should not be practiced for its own sake.

Thus, a manager should have an in-depth understanding of the organization's identity, strategy, and culture before embarking on knowledge management. Just like any other management activity, KM must contribute to an organization's core mission. Moreover, the manager's vision should be compatible with that of other key individuals in an organization so that the manager's enthusiasm for knowledge management will be shared. Gathering support and enthusiasm from like-minded colleagues significantly improves the chances of success of any managerial intervention.

Assess Your Organization

We recommend starting with some kind of an assessment of the current organizational state of affairs with regard to knowledge management. This assessment should not be overly extensive or complicated; it should merely serve to give you an indication of your starting point. If you are a senior manager, this task can be delegated to others. If you do delegate, make sure that the assessment is not overdone. Over analysis can lead to paralysis, and in this case it is not necessary. The assessment should serve as a basis for deriving goals and objectives about where you want to go relative to where you are today.

Derive Intellectual Capital Goals

An organization's strategy is the source for deriving IC goals, for which a few simple indicators should be selected to serve as guidelines. Chapter 9 outlined how you derive IC goals and indicators. This is a very important step for the following reasons.

Committing to IC goals may be an important revolution for some organizations and managers. Usually, every manager is occupied with day-to-day operations and/or financial results. Realizing the importance of IC, and making some long-term commitments, is the first step in KM after you have defined your strategy and vision.

Hence, we recommend looking at all the various Navigator focus areas (or the relevant sections in the Balanced Scorecard) and defining at least one important indicator for each of them. This is necessary to make yourself and your organization begin thinking in terms of long-term and intangible intellectual capital. To make this change in state of mind easier, you might want to begin with some indicators that are already taken care of in some way at your organization.

Here we would like to emphasize a key point: Simplicity is golden. An overabundance of indicators creates unnecessary noise. Moreover, if you are focused in your efforts and other organizational members perceive this focus, they will appreciate your seriousness. This is particularly important, as you must carefully avoid initial failures. A few wrong steps at the beginning may lead to negative results that generate cynicism and resistance from others. An important way to ensure initial success is to be focused on the most relevant and important issues when choosing your indicators.

Begin with Pilots

Once a vision and clear objectives are in place, it is time to implement a few pilots. By recruiting a few like-minded people, you can improve the chances of success of these pilots. When there is a vision that gets people excited, they will volunteer to participate. This becomes a self-organizing process.

You can choose your pilots from the various chapters of the book according to the needs you identified and the goals you set. You may choose pilots that promote interactions, focus on capturing, learn from customers, and so on. Those pilots that succeed should be copied and repeated throughout the organization. As for unsuccessful pilots, do not be deterred. Some setbacks are inevitable.

Start Small

In this book, we have shared with you a large repertoire of examples, problems, and solutions in knowledge management. To increase the likelihood of success, we suggest that you do not attempt to implement them all at once. There are many types of knowledge management practices, but we suggest that you start with some carefully chosen projects. It is of utmost importance that you choose the appropriate methods for your organization, based on the analysis you conduct. Remember, sometimes less is more.

Begin with changes that have the following characteristics:

1. High potential contribution.
2. High likelihood of successful implementation.

If these two guidelines are followed, then you and other members of your organization will feel the impact of the changes you implement. The benefit of the knowledge management tool will be appreciated. This will happen relatively quickly because the interventions you chose to begin with had a high likelihood of success. This initial success will engender the energy to implement more KM methods and upgrade the level of knowledge management in the organization.

The paramount guideline should be simplicity. While beginning, adopt a pilot approach; do not undertake a revolution. Stick to small interventions with a high likelihood of success, otherwise you will face an insurmountable wall of resistance. The revolution will develop after accumulation of enough small successes.

Also, be sure you do not make the common mistake of equating knowledge management with knowledge capturing. This tendency is especially tempting in light of the various software vendors that offer sophisticated products that are not necessarily practical. An overemphasis on knowledge capturing often leads to oversight of the cultural issues that enable effective knowledge capturing, as described in Chapters 4 and 7.

We are not saying that knowledge capturing is not a worthwhile knowledge management activity. In fact, knowledge capturing is important for many organizations, particularly *long-tech* organizations, such as in the aerospace and pharmaceutical industries. But overemphasizing knowledge capturing processes may come at the price of knowledge creation, renewal, and innovation. Capturing is important mainly as an enabler for innovation. Chapter 10 on innovation has emphasized this point.

Who Should Do It

The initiator of knowledge management does not have to be a senior manager. He does, however, have to be an entrepreneur, a person with initiative who knows how to create a coalition and get people excited.

The Initiator

If you are a manager of a small organization or a unit within a large organization, we suggest you begin by doing it yourself, or delegate it to someone who has proximity to the subject, such as the R&D manager. What is important is that the person you recruit to initiate knowledge management should have a passion for the topic—otherwise it is doomed to fail.

If you do delegate someone to lead the knowledge management, this does not mean that you are exempt from practicing it yourself. You, the manager, should still be the leader of knowledge management implementation in your organization. The junior manager who assumes responsibility should receive your guidance, and your joint efforts should focus on attaining small successes. These initial outcomes can be used to sell the concept of knowledge management to senior management.

Chief Knowledge Officers

The CEO of a large organization should delegate the task of initiating knowledge management to a project manager and eventually appoint a permanent chief knowledge officer (CKO). The existence of a CKO has a symbolic significance to the organization. It sends the message that knowledge is an important asset that merits a manager, just like other important resources (financial, human, information, etc.). Many organizations have chosen to begin managing knowledge in this way.

Knowledge managers can rise from various backgrounds. You should identify people with enthusiasm for the subject and nurture it:

- Knowledge managers can come from a financial background, which implies that their activities would focus on measuring the knowledge of the organization.
- They can come from the information systems field, which means that they would contribute to the organization's technological position in the knowledge community.
- They can come from human resources, which would help them recruit and motivate knowledge workers to share their knowledge with others.
- Former R&D workers may focus on developing organizational memory, since they know better than anyone the price of reinventing the wheel. Former external consultants can develop knowledge products that can be sold to smaller organizations that cannot afford a full-time knowledge manager.

Summarizing, knowledge management has the potential to be practiced in a number of different ways and can rise from a variety of organizational functions. Remember to exhibit continuous and consistent support of your CKO.

Consultants

If you choose to employ management consultants, make sure you have a clear understanding of their role. Consultants are most effective when they are catalysts, sources of additional points of view and perspectives through their familiarity with many organizations, and as the coaches of the relevant people. Management consultants should not be expected to manage your knowledge for you. Since knowledge management is one of the core processes, activities, and values of the organization, it should be embedded within its work processes.

The Final Goal

Ultimately, our final goal is to help you make knowledge management an inseparable part of the organizational culture, of the work processes, and of the information systems. Successful implementation of knowledge management implies that it becomes a self-sustaining cultural aspect of your organization.

Of course, our goal has been to advocate knowledge management and provide the basic tools for its implementation. However, we would like to sign off by emphasizing that knowledge management should be practiced carefully. The methods should not be simultaneously applied, as it is important to begin with small steps that will lead to initial successes. Building on these successes, these steps will gradually get bigger and stronger, until you are striding confidently alongside the leading knowledge-managing companies.

Defining Key Terms

As we stated in the Preface, this book is primarily about knowledge and intellectual capital, and we have used the terms freely without asserting exact definitions. While expecting that many readers already have a good idea of the basic definitions of these terms, we want to give a bit more context so you can comprehend the terms as you read through the chapters.

Levels of Knowledge

Knowledge is composed of several components that lie on a continuum, shown in Figure A.1. Each level is defined in the following paragraphs, in order to show you how the definitions specifically apply to knowledge management.

Data and Information

Data is the raw material of knowledge management. It is at the base of the entire process. When you process this raw material—and today it is

FIGURE A.1 Levels of Knowledge

possible to process it using various technological systems—it becomes *information*. Information is processed data. But the information you end up with still does not address whatever managerial problems you face.

To illustrate, think of data and information in this metaphor, regarding solving a medical problem of a patient:

The Medical Metaphor, Part I: Data and Information

A patient with a medical problem may have the data and/or information about a specific medication. The *data* about the medication is the drug's chemical composition, other characteristics discovered through its development, or some therapeutic indications. The data may be assembled as *information* in the leaflet that is packaged with the drug when you pick up your prescription.

However, neither the data nor the information (the leaflet) is usually relevant to the cure sought by the patient taking the medication. The patient simply wants to know which medication will cure his bad symptoms.

In a business environment, endless data may be assembled into abundant information about the overall status of a company, but it is not sufficient on its own to determine whether a company's management situation is bad or good, and what action to take. Coming to conclusions about the data and picking a direction to travel in to solve business issues requires additional experience and expertise.

Knowledge

To actually solve a problem backed up by data, you need to go up a level. We call this level, above data and information, *knowledge*. The existence or lack of knowledge is put to the test only through action. When there is a problem, there are those who know how to solve it and those who do not know how to solve it. They either have the knowledge or they don't.

Of course, those who have the knowledge need information to solve the problem, but the information is not enough. They need more. Solving the problem requires experience and expertise, which, when joined with the data and information, becomes knowledge. In the medical metaphor:

The Medical Metaphor, Part II: Knowledge

In our example of medication for a patient, we usually think of the physician as the one with the knowledge. Told about the symptoms and other information within the patient's medical profile, he can solve the problem and take action to suggest an appropriate medication. If the problem is complicated, the physician may consult with colleagues who can share their knowledge with him or refer him to knowledge in books or available via the Internet.

In modern times, the example becomes more sophisticated and more instructive. Nowadays the physician is not the only one with the knowledge. Intelligent patients are usually quite aware of their own body and medical history. Also, they have probably searched the Internet extensively to study their problems upon first symptoms.

So sometimes the patient may already have the knowledge to take action, and choose a specific medication in response to the problem. Other times the patient still has to seek the help of a medical professional. If the two parties are open and cooperative, their interaction will create new knowledge helpful for everyone involved, and not only in terms of that specific patient, but future patients for that doctor.

The implications for the organizational environment are many but obvious. We have already mentioned that knowledge is required to take action on the facts that data presents. This medical example demonstrates important processes of knowledge sharing, knowledge dissemination, and, most importantly, knowledge creation.

Intellectual Capital and Wisdom

But you can climb up yet another level. The next level is *intellectual capital.* Intellectual capital is the intangible asset that combines the knowledge of an organization as a whole—the knowledge the employees possess (human capital) and the ensemble of established work processes, customer knowledge, and so forth (structural capital). It complements the tangible financial capital of data and information.

In brief, we can say that it is knowledge management and intellectual capital that creates for an organization the potential for future growth, future success, and future earnings. Knowledge is the core competence of an organization that can be strategically managed for organizational success. But it is *wisdom* (the ability to identify which knowledge has the potential to be intellectual capital) that is worth investing in and developing because there are good chances that it will generate the future's most desired outcomes.

The concept of wisdom is related to a high sensitivity in the organization to what is happening in the external environment—its opportunities and threats. The utilization of knowledge to take advantage of opportunities is what makes an organization wise. Wisdom describes an organization that renews its knowledge continuously; an organization with high intellectual capital and potential for future growth.

We conclude the medical metaphor to illustrate Intellectual Capital:

The Medication Metaphor, Part III: Intellectual Capital

In the previous medical example, intellectual capital would be associated with a medical institution, like a clinic or hospital. It obviously consists of the combined professional expertise of all its physicians, utilized for continued improvement of the medical treatment of patients (human capital). But it also entails other expertise—for example, the administrative skills and work processes of countless departments and colleagues in the efficient operation of the hospital (structural capital).

Conclusion

While this book is mainly about knowledge and intellectual capital, this Appendix aims to put various levels of knowledge into context for the reader, and also serves as an alternate approach for introducing the subject. The topics of data and information are respectable disciplines by themselves, and there is vast literature available on them if readers would like to continue their research.

Notes

Chapter 1—The Motivation toward Knowledge Management

1. Gary Hammel and C. K. Prahalad, *Competing for the Future* (Boston: Harvard Business School Press, 1994).
2. "Holon, the Children City, Jumped Ahead," *Haaretz* and TheMarker .com, August 21, 2008.
3. "Ten Mayors: The Urban Politicians Transforming Their Cities and Inspiring Others," *Monocle*, issue 35, volume 04, July/August 2010.
4. Leif Edvinsson and Michael S. Malone, *Intellectual Capital: Realizing Your Company's True Value by Finding its Hidden Brainpower* (New York: HarperCollins, 1997).
5. Thomas A. Stewart, *Intellectual Capital: The New Wealth of Organizations* (New York: Currency Books, 1997). *The Wealth of Knowledge: Intellectual Capital and the Twenty-First Century Organization* (New York: Currency Books, 2001).
6. Dan Senor and Saul Singer, *Start-Up Nation: The Story of Israel's Economic Miracle* (New York: Hachette Book Group, Twelve, 2009).
7. Ibid.

Chapter 2—Making the Business Case for Managing Intellectual Capital

1. Leif Edvinsson, then vice president for Intellectual Capital at Skandia, interview in Skandia HQ in Stockholm, June 1997.
2. *Israel State Comptroller Annual Report*, 1997 (in Hebrew).
3. Zehavit Cohen, chairperson of the board of Tnuva, lecture in the "Leadership Agenda" conference, organized by The Interdisciplinary Center (IDC), Herzliya, Israel, March 2010.
4. Baruch Lev, "Sharpening the Intangibles Edge," *Harvard Business Review*, June 2004.

5. Ibid.
6. Annie Brooking, *Intellectual Capital: Core Asset for the Third Millennium Enterprise* (London: International Thomson Business Press, 1996). Brooking cites evidence of the UK Accounting Standards Board, surveying acquisitions in the United Kingdom, that the amount paid for "purchased goodwill"—an overarching name for intangible assets—as percentage of the net worth grew from 1 percent of market value in 1976 to 44 percent in 1987.
7. Edvinsson, interview.
8. Lev, "Sharpening."
9. Ibid.
10. Robert Kaplan and David Norton, *Balanced Scorecard: Translating Strategy into Action* (Boston: Harvard Business School Press, 1996); and Robert Kaplan and David Norton, *Strategy Maps: Converting Intangible Assets into Tangible Outcomes* (Boston: Harvard Business School Press, 2004).
11. Leif Edvinsson and Michael S. Malone, *Intellectual Capital: Realizing Your Company's True Value by Finding its Hidden Brainpower* (New York: HarperCollins, 1997).
12. Ibid.
13. Henrik Danckwardt, then CFO of AFS (a subsidiary of Skandia), interview in Skandia headquarters in Stockholm, June 1997.
14. Lev, "Sharpening."
15. Kaplan and Norton, *Balanced Scorecard*.
16. Edvinsson, interview.

Chapter 3—The Importance of Strategy in Knowledge Management

1. Gary Hamel and C. K. Prahalad, *Competing for the Future* (Boston: Harvard Business School Press, 1994).
2. Patrick Sullivan, *Value-Driven Intellectual Capital: How to Convert Intangible Corporate Assets into Market Value* (New York: John Wiley & Sons, 2000).
3. Izzy Borovich, talk in a "round-table conversation on innovation management" published in *Status* magazine, Israel, May 2010.
4. Joseph Shoval, External Communications Manager of IBM Israel, written communication, April 2010.
5. Barbara Opall-Rome, "From Pauper to Powerhouse: Israeli Firm Profits from Successful Transformation," *Defense News*, April 26, 2010.
6. Rafael mission statement, Rafael web site, www.rafael.co.il.
7. Opall-Rome, "From Pauper to Powerhouse."

8. The following are classic books on strategic management: Gary Hamel, *Leading the Revolution* (Boston: Harvard Business School Press, 2000); James Collins and Jerry Porras, *Built to Last: Successful Habits of Visionary Companies* (New York: Harper Business, 1997); James Collins, *Good to Great* (New York: HarperBusiness, 2001); Arie de Geus, *The Living Company: Growth, Learning and Longevity in Business* (London: Nicholas Brealey, 1997).

Chapter 4—The Role of Culture in a Successful Knowledge-Creating and Knowledge-Sharing Organization

1. Patrick Sullivan, *Value-Driven Intellectual Capital: How to Convert Intangible Corporate Assets into Market Value* (New York: John Wiley & Sons, 2000).
2. Barbara Opall-Rome, "From Pauper to Powerhouse: Israeli Firm Profits from Successful Transformation," *Defense News*, April 26, 2010.
3. Bonee Tirosh, *"The Story of Cross-Israel Highway, 1995–2004"* (Israel: Derech Eretz Construction Joint Venture, December 2004).
4. Sullivan, *Value-Driven Intellectual Capital.*
5. Eugene S. Meierman, Intel fellow, interview in Santa Clara, California, July 1997. Similar ideas were conveyed by Maxin Fasnberg, manager of Intel Israel, in a presentation in January 2010.
6. Ichak Adizes, lecture in the "Leadership Agenda" conference, organized by The Interdisciplinary Center (IDC), Herzliya, Israel, March 2010.
7. More information about BP's peer assist system and the overall management strategy it represents can be found in the following sources: Morten T. Hansen and Bolko von Oetinger, "Introducing T-Shaped Managers: Knowledge Management's Next Generation," *Harvard Business Review*, March 2001, 107–116; Chris Collison and Geoff Parcell, *Learning to Fly: Practical Lessons from one of the World's Leading Knowledge Companies* (Capstone Publishing, 2001).
8. Hansen and von Oetinger, "Introducing T-Shaped Managers."

Chapter 5—The Human Focus

1. Susan Stucky, IRL manager, interview in Menlo Park, California, July 1997.
2. Brigitte Jordan, *Technology and Social Interaction: Notes on the Achievement of Authoritative Knowledge in Complex Settings*, IRL Technical Report No. IRL92-0027 (Palo Alto, CA: Institute for Research on Learning, 1992).

3. *Israel State Comptroller Annual Report*, 1997 (in Hebrew).
4. Amos Shapira, president and CEO of Cellcom Israel Ltd., lecture in the "Leadership Agenda" conference, organized by The Interdisciplinary Center (IDC), Herzliya, Israel, March 2010.
5. Bipin Junnarkar, former head of knowledge management architecture at Monsanto, interview in Monsanto headquarters, Saint Louis, Missouri, May 1997.
6. Patricia Seemann, former director of knowledge management at Hoffmann-La Roche Pharmaceuticals, interview in Zurich, Switzerland, May 1997.

Chapter 6—Managing Interactions for Knowledge Creation and Sharing

1. Bipin Junnarkar, former head of knowledge management architecture in Monsanto, interview in Monsanto headquarters, Saint Louis, Missouri, May 1997.
2. Ibid.
3. Patricia Seemann, former director of knowledge management at Hoffmann-La Roche Pharmaceuticals, interview in Zurich, Switzerland, May 1997.
4. Peter Himes, former director of technology programs at NSC (leading KM initiatives), interview in Palo Alto, California, July 1997.
5. Ibid.
6. Juanita Brown, consultant, interview in Mill Valley, California, May 1997.
7. Rony Dayan, Edna Pasher, and Ron Dvir, "The Knowledge Management Journey of Israel Aircraft Industry," a case study in the book *Real Life Knowledge Management: Lessons from the Field* (KnowledgeBoard, 2006).
8. Himes, interview.
9. Seemann, interview.
10. The World Café online community, www.theworldcafe.com.
11. IBM Jam events web site, https://www.collaborationjam.com/. Accessed 2008.

Chapter 7—Capturing and Reusing Knowledge

1. Patricia Seemann, former director of knowledge systems at Hoffmann-La Roche Pharmaceuticals, interview in Zurich, Switzerland, May 1997; and Patricia Seemann, "A Prescription for Knowledge Management,"

Innovation in Action, www.providersedge.com/docs/km_articles/A_Prescription_for_KM.pdf.

2. Arian Ward, then leader of collaboration, knowledge, and learning at Hughes, together with Kailash Kapur and Dan Huang, then two team leaders in engineering group at Hughes Space and Communications Company (HSC), interview in Hughes headquarters in El Segundo, California, July 1997. Note: HSC was acquired by Boeing in 2000 to become Boeing Satellite Development Center (SDC).
3. Peter Himes, former leader of KM initiatives at NSC, interview in Palo Alto, California, July 1997.
4. National Semiconductor web site, http://www.national.com/analog/training. Accessed 2010.
5. Ward, Kapur, and Huang, interview.
6. Eugene S. Meierman, Intel Fellow, interview in Santa Clara, July 1997.
7. Maxin Fasnberg, manager of Intel Israel, presentation during a visit in Intel FAB in Israel, January 2010.

Chapter 8—The Customer Focus

1. Links to wearit@work and Living Labs at the EU: www.wearitatwork.com, www.ami-communities.eu/drupal/node/28.
2. "Chromatis Closed," Ynet, an Israeli news web site, August 2001; www.ynet.co.il/articles/0,7340,L-1059929,00.html.

Chapter 9—Measuring and Managing the Performance of Proper Knowledge Work

1. Baruch Lev, "Sharpening the Intangibles Edge," *Harvard Business Review*, June 2004.
2. Ibid.
3. Henrik Danckwardt, then CFO of AFS (a subsidiary of Skandia), interview in Skandia HQ in Stockholm, June 1997.
4. Leif Edvinsson, then vice president for Intellectual Capital at Skandia, interview at Skandia headquarters in Stockholm, June 1997.
5. Danckwardt, interview.
6. Madeleine Jarehov, Caroline Stenfelt, and Andres Ericsson, *Welfare and Security for Future Generations: The Intellectual Capital of Sweden* (Stockholm: Market Academy, Stockholm University, 1997).
7. Edna Pasher et al., *The Intellectual Capital Balance Sheet of the State of Israel—1998* (Tel Aviv: Edna Pasher and Associates, 1998).

8. Edna Pasher et al., *The Intellectual Capital of the State of Israel—2007*, 3rd ed. (Jerusalem: Office of the Chief Scientist of the Ministry of Industry, Trade and Labor, 2007).

Chapter 10—Innovating for a New Beginning

1. Data retrieved from various sources: newspaper interview with Dadi Perlmuter, Intel VP, in *Haaretz* and The Marker.com, May 13, 2010; and Intel web site (www.intel.com), May 2010.
2. Barbara Opall-Rome, "From Pauper to Powerhouse: Israeli Firm Profits from Successful Transformation," *Defense News*, April 26, 2010.
3. Dan Senor and Saul Singer, *Start-Up Nation: The Story of Israel's Economic Miracle* (New York: Hachette Book Group, Twelve, 2009).
4. Tuvya Ronen and Edna Pasher, unpublished draft about Applied Materials, October 2001.
5. From *Haaretz* daily newspaper, February 2002.
6. "Applied Materials Lays Off 60 to 80 Employees in Israel," *Maariv* daily newspaper, October 31, 2002.
7. Applied Materials financial data in its web site, http://www.appliedmaterials.com/investors/. Accessed July 2010.
8. Yossi Ackerman, Elbit CEO, TheMarker.com newspaper interview, February 2010.
9. Leif Edvinsson, then vice president for Intellectual Capital at Skandia, interview in Skandia headquarters in Stockholm, June 1997.
10. James C. Collins and Jerry I. Porras, *Built to Last: Successful Habits of Visionary Companies* (New York: HarperBusiness, 1995).

Index